Building a House: The Perspective from the Foundation

Building a Relationship-The Perspective from the Individual

Building a Life-The Perspective from the Spirit

Maceo M. NeSmith III

All rights reserved. This book and parts thereof may not be reproduced in any form, or transmitted in any form by any means, (Electronic, mechanical, photocopying, or otherwise) without prior written permission of the author.

All names that appear in this book have been changed for privacy reasons.

Copyright © 2012 by Maceo M. NeSmith III
PRINTED IN THE UNITED STATES FIRST PRINTING

SEPTEMBER 2012 ISBN-13: 978-0615688251

ISBN-10: 061568825X

Acknowledgements

I thank everyone that I've created and shared experiences with. I've learned a lot from every single one of my experiences. I especially thank Professor Derwin Campbell (Humanities & English Professor) from Morgan State University for his assistance in transitioning my thoughts on to paper. A special thanks to my good friends: Brian F. Antoniak, Morris W. Ricks Sr, Robert "Chef" White, and Lavaugn Leach.

TABLE OF CONTENTS
Chapter 1: Real Estate-1
    Society's Misdirection's
    Dating
Chapter 2: Survey Foundation Site-40
    Importance of Foundation
Chapter 3: Construction Failures-70
    Learning from past relationships
    Cheating
Chapter 4: Framework-106
    Emotions
    Communication
Chapter 5: External vs. Internal View-175
    Priorities 1 & 2
    Discriminators
Chapter 6: Foundation of Happiness-204
    Definition of happiness
    Internal happiness
        VS.
    External happiness
Chapter 7: Purpose-Built-233
Chapter 8: Family Foundation-244
Chapter 9: Different Foundations
(Epilogue)-261

The problems that exist in the world cannot be solved by the level of thinking that created them.

                                             Albert Einstein

Chapter 1. Real Estate

I do not possess a Ph. D, a Master's degree, a Bachelor's degree or even an Associate's degree, but what I do possess is a perception of life specifically on relationships that may be helpful on your journey. We sometimes have a feeling deep inside us that yearns for a connection with someone else. I know I'm not the only one that felt that before. The connection can be explained in any number of ways: through psychology, religion, science, etc; however, I will not touch on any of those.

In order to fully satisfy that yearning we must focus inwards at our foundation. Our best way to understand our experiences is to analyze ourselves. We learn about ourselves through acknowledging our connections to our experiences.

The connection to the experiences holds the answers to our many questions that we seek in the outer world, or we ask to ourselves. All of our experiences, positive or negative, we can learn from. If we can take the time to step back from an experience, look at it from a different angle, we can walk away with knowledge. It is that knowledge that assists us on our individual paths of life or can be of assistance to someone who crosses our path. That is the birth of wisdom that we so commonly speak of in our conversations. Wisdom is the application of knowledge that is gained through our experiences whether they were directly or vicariously related to us.

Wisdom is not the quantity of experiences-that we commonly correlate with age. It is merely the quality of the knowledge that was obtained from the experiences. Sometimes when we are in our experiences we only have the perspective from our eyes. Our perception can be considered a "Bittersweet" moment; in such that what we see is what registers to us that enables us to learn from the experience or do the complete opposite and not learn.

However, when we shift our perspective on an experience it has the ability to shed light on a specific lesson or knowledge that can be obtained. It's very similar to looking at a slide through a microscope with no lens magnification and seeing nothing. Once I change the lens I began to see something, which I normally couldn't have seen.

Our lives are filled with many changes,

which are dependent on the choices we make, but one of our constants in life is our perception. How we evaluate our perception of an experience is based on how we define our lives. How we define our lives is based on the perception of our experiences. Our perception of an experience "Sets the Stage" for our emotions, knowledge, and future experiences to follow.

We have many ways on which we define our lives and how we live our lives. A few of them include: astrology, religion, spirituality, etc. With or without these guides, we still need to step back and focus inwards. Inside of all of us is a place that wants to be found, a place that cannot be reached through our outward journey. The type of place that wants to answer all of our questions, but can only be reached by us and through us.

This type of place is not concerned with our temporary 'Joy' from our materialistic possessions. This place does not judge us on our habitual mistakes. All this place wants to do is: bring stillness to our minds, enlighten us from our experiences, patch up our hearts and allow us to enjoy life from the inside to the out.

Occasionally, life will throw a curveball that forces us to go inwards to understand what is going on outwards. When this happens people usually say, "I need to find myself." It is not so much that people need to find themselves, but more so that people need to understand how they're connected to what happens outwardly. For instance, our experiences from our relationships have a wealth of knowledge once we shift our perspective. Ever notice how our perceptions of our relationships are different once we learn from them?

I've had a few people that have crossed my path and one of the main questions that I'm always asked is, "Why are you single?" The tone of the question sounds like being single is like a disease. Usually that question is in comparison to being in a relationship that leads to marriage and having a family. When did it become "Single vs. Relationship (marriage and family)"?

For some odd reason if one is single, one is wrong; however, if one is in a relationship one is right. What I think is interesting is that some people who hate being single, will choose to be in an unhealthy relationship, just to be in a relationship. To this day I will never understand why people choose to be in an unhealthy relationship or hate being single. But of course I will take a stab at trying to understand why people choose to do so. One of the most frequent words that I hear in conversations about being single is loneliness. Feeling lonely happens to be a common reason why some people hate being single and choose to be in an unhealthy relationship. What exactly is wrong with being alone? I do not think the problem is so much of being alone, but more so on what we have associated with being by ourselves.

Take holidays for instance, by ourselves we do not have anyone there for us to spend our time with. We have no one to send flowers to us for Valentine's Day or go out for a movie and dinner. Nor do we have anyone to watch the firework display on the fourth of July or watch the ball drop in Time square.

We cannot forget the seasonal outings that occur throughout the year. Of course we have no one to go to the beach with us or take a cruise to the Bahamas. We have no one to attend the annual fall festival with us, which blocks off every street in a three-block radius. We have no one to ice skate with hand-in-hand or snuggle up with on winter evenings to watch a movie.

These examples are just the tip of the iceberg on what we may associate with being alone. What about the other entity that is associated with being alone? Like being able to develop a stronger self-relationship. Could it be possible that the lonely feeling that we may feel could be stemming from the inner-self wanting a relationship too? Or is it only possible to cure the loneliness feeling by being with someone else?

The majority of the focus in society is that of the "Outward" focus. Who can I be with to make my life better? Can I find someone that can make my life more complete? The time that we have to ourselves aka lonely can be used to build our individual self-relationships. If we have a relationship with self, then how are we lonely? The society that we live in today makes it quite clear that if we do not have anyone by our sides then we are lonely. For example, if a person doesn't have a "Valentine" for Valentines Day, or a person to go with us out in town. Society does not understand that a self- relationship doesn't mean a person is lonely.

Earlier when I mentioned those that hate being alone choose to be in an unhealthy relationship, I was stating the truth. The people who fall under this category get into a relationship for the wrong reasons. These people want to find someone who will not make them feel lonely anymore. The example below will demonstrate an unhealthy relationship:

Person A is lonely and gets in a relationship with Person B because he or she "Really like's" Person B and will not be lonely anymore.

Person B had a few changes in his/her employment and now works more hours during the week, than when Person B met Person A.

Person A is noticing that Person B is spending less and less time with him/her.

So Person A is starting to feel lonely while being in a relationship with Person B.

At this point, this is usually when trouble arises

and when Person A becomes more "Friendly" with others; to the point where Person A feels distant from Person B and has found a new person that shows him/her attention.

Person A starts to wonder why he/she is still in a relationship with Person B.

We all know the ending to this story. Person A is a prime example of the type of person who chooses to be in a relationship to not only cure loneliness, but an entire array of things. I find it ironic that Person A needed a relationship to not feel alone, and in the relationship he or she still felt alone. If before and during a relationship one feels alone, then most likely that comes from not having a self- relationship.

On the other hand, imagine if Person A developed a stronger self-relationship. When he or she had the "Lonely feeling", he or she turned inwards instead of outwards. He or she chose to ask, "Why do I feel lonely or why do I want to be with someone"? With these types of questions Person A, is able to dig deeper to understand where the lonely feeling is stemming from. Person A goes on an inward journey to reconnect with him or herself. Person A learns to be content with being by him or herself while still being able to enjoy life.

Now if Person A decides to be in a relationship with Person B, Person A will know how to show himself or herself attention. He or she will not DEPEND on Person B to be with them 24/7- 365 days a year. Spending time with Person B is always great, but it will not be the building blocks for the relationship. Meaning these two people can build a stronger foundation with some depth. There are some of us out here who constantly feel in competition with someone else. Especially when it comes to having a steady healthy relationship. We feel the need to compare our individual lives to others, whether we know them or not. For instance, we may notice that we're the only ones out of a group, who's single or in an unhealthy relationship. We may even say to ourselves "Why I am I the only one out of... to be single? Or why am I the only one who is always in an unhealthy relationship?"

The problem with comparing ourselves to others, once again, is the perception issue and the patience issue. Each one of our experiences has a lesson for us to learn. We may see a "Happy Couple" and wonder why we cannot be in their shoes. We are in no position to compare ourselves to someone else's relationship. When we do make comparisons we only perceive what we observe.

Society's Misdirection of Support

Have you ever heard someone say: "You know I support you in anything you choose to do or I'll always be in your corner. I've heard everything on this list at least once in my life. These are one of the many generic "Societal Definitions" that some of us say when we want to express to others that we support them one hundred percent. However, are the above examples really supportive to those that need support? When I've thought long and hard on a subject and I reach a fork in the road, I expect the other person to give an opinion, not the generic response. The reason we ask our significant others, is due to the fact that they're outside of us and can sometimes see things that we may not see for ourselves. For example, say there is a couple by the names of Bob and Susan. Bob is an electrical engineer and is considering pursing a Master's program in engineering management. Bob has thought about it and is having difficulty making a decision. So Bob asks Susan what she thinks. Susan's replies to Bob:

Society's definition of support: "Bob you know I'll always be in your corner and I'll support whichever decision you choose." Bob gives her a kiss on the forehead and says "Thanks Susan". Inside of Bob's head he is saying, "I'm still at square one and I do not know what to do".

The Real Definition of support: "Bob this program paired with your experience makes you marketable if there are any management/leadership openings in the future. There really isn't any downside to pursing this program."

The first definition of support follows the typical response for those that want to be supportive. People give responses that really do not help the ones who may be at a fork in the road. The second response is what I consider to be the real definition of support. Susan is able to help Bob make a better decision due to her analysis of Bob's situation and knowing the qualities that Bob possesses. The "Real" definition of support may not always be positive;

I just used a positive example to prove a point.

Imagine there are two large pieces of land adjacent to each other with two sets of builders waiting idly by, to build a single-family house. The first set of builders are extremely excited to start building because of visualizing the final appearance, based on all the other house's they've seen. They can picture the house already built with: a sixty inch roof mounted basketball hoop above the garage, eight foot deep twenty meter swimming pool, fifty inch plasma flat screen in the family room, Afyon black marble countertops, and a spacious sunroom with java wicker chairs. Without anymore thought they jump right into building the walls of their future house.

Now, turn your focus to the other set of builders. They visualize the same appearance as the first set of builders, except with a slightly different focus. They do imagine those amenities too just it is not the main focus when it comes to building a house. Wisdom from life experiences has shown them that without a strong-solid foundation, a house will never stand. When nature allows a storm to pass, the house with the strongest foundation has a higher chance of survival. **And the houses that were built by those who were oblivious to building the foundation, will not survive any of Mother Nature's storms.**

These two examples of building a house directly correlate with the two types of approaches to relationships. The first set of builders represents the type of people who are entirely focused on the "Final Look" or

"Benefits" of a relationship. For the most part they want to emulate the type of relationships they've observed. The reason for them wanting the relationship is due to what is associated with being in a relationship. Those that approach relationships in this manner are focused primarily on the surface.

The second set of builders represents the type of people who understand that one cannot build a relationship without a strong foundation. Before he or she can even fathom what his or her relationship could be like he or she must know what is at the foundation. These builders understand the whole house will be resting on the foundation. Prior to working jointly on the foundation, he or she must know what is at their individual foundations. Two people who come together with different individual foundations will run into conflict trying to build with an uneven foundation. Of course, those that have no foundation will not be able to build a house. In other words, if two people come together to build a relationship they must have established a connection at the foundation.

Many of us yearn for that "Special Relationship" without games, confusion, miscommunication, etc; and there is nothing wrong with that. It's just something wrong with the mindset that we have to get there. The answers that we have beneath the surface of what a relationship should be are not compatible with the approach on the surface.

For instance, our approach for dating does not match what we're looking for (Beneath the surface). Dates should be more concentrated on compatibility and which places are suited for conversations. Conversations are how we communicate and determine compatibility. Why is taking or meeting someone at the movies so popular for the first couple of dates? Think about it, dating is about determining compatibility with another person.

If it's because one is on a budget, one can go to a park for free and get more out of date than the movies. One may also think it's about enjoying his or her company, but I'll touch on that shortly. So why do people go on dates to places where there is no dialogue? Movies, nightclubs, concerts, etc, are not the ideal locations for first dates, if you're "Getting to know someone".

Locations for dates should be at places where one can hear each other speak as well as being able to hear one think. If one has to shout or lean over so his or her mouth is directly over a person's ear, then that is the wrong place for a date. If I'm at a movie theater with someone depending on the genre, there may be tears, laughs, yells, etc but no conversation. Here's a question, if people go to the movies on the first date to enjoy a person's company, how exactly does that happen? We do not know the person well enough to know if we will even enjoy his or her company.

Personally, when I want get to know a person and I have the choice on where the date is, I want to take her to an interactive and engaging environment that allows conversation to take place. A part of my individual foundation is an inquisitive mind with an everlasting thirst for learning; as well as, enjoying mental stimulation in the form of conversation. For me, life is about learning and there is so much to learn. There is always something new to learn and I'm never going to know everything. Anyways, I like to go to bookstores, aquariums, museums, etc. What these places have in common is that they're perfect for conversations and they are very stimulating environments.

I'm always curious to know if my date will be stuck on my hip or will my date venture off: to another section of the bookstore, stray off to look at other sea life, or read the inscriptions of a piece of art. This isn't a game or anything of that nature, but a way for me to see if she has other interests or if she is only interested in what I'm interested in.

When I'm on a date, I ask thought provoking questions. I may ask, "What are your observations about life?" When I ask questions I sincerely want to know, I do not just ask to make pointless conversation. On a side note, I can't understand how someone who is alive has trouble answering a question about observing life.

As I stated previously I like mental stimulation, and thought provoking questions/subjects are an interest for me. I absolutely hate yes or no answers, I always want to know why. The reason for that is "Why" questions always provide so much more depth into who the person is. Also, by asking those types of questions it enables me to see if my date can effectively articulate her thoughts and feelings. Hence, why I dislike yes or no answers. I prefer to ask "Yes or No" questions after I have connected with a woman beneath the surface. By the way, yes or no questions are what I call "Surface Questions". Why? The answer to "Surface Questions", stay right on the surface and have no depth.

Have you ever been in a relationship and started to notice things about someone that you didn't like? When you ask them why/how long they've been doing it, they say, "I've always done this or I've always been like this". Then most likely you say to yourself or to them, "You didn't do that when we first started dating or you weren't like that when I met you". These situations usually happen because of our approaches to dating. That is the most frustrating experience, you thought you finally had a great connection but that one flaw ruined the relationship.

Nowadays, two people go on 8 dates (figuratively speaking) and they become "Official" and off the market. His or her dates were comprised of: movies, concerts, nightclubs, sport events, and going to dinner.

He or she tells their friends: Ex.1

I'm so glad I finally met someone; we have so much in common. Both of us like the same types of movies, he or she loves to listen to… We saw them in concert last Saturday. He or she loves to dance and has even shown me some new moves. I finally found a man or woman that I can go to football games with. He or she isn't afraid to try different cuisines just like me. This is just the tip of the iceberg, he or she is ambitious, focused, spiritually based, mature, thoughtful, and loves to make me laugh. He or she is the one!!!

Eight dates, one month later:

> I just don't understand him or her; he or she acted mature when we first met, now he or she acts like a child. He or she flirts with every man or woman that's around us. He or she doesn't make time for me anymore; all he or she cares about is their job. Our dates aren't even exciting anymore. I just do not know what happened with us.

Our conversations that we have with our friends or our inner circle are somewhat along the lines of the examples above. Do these examples sound familiar? The way in which we approach dates

(Including locations) and the types of questions asked are the reasons we end up like the above examples. The approach to dating is bass-ackwards, which is why "Time has to fly by" before we ask ourselves, "Who is this person?" We should be asking, "Who is this person" on day one, not day 31. Society including those so-called "Relationship Experts" has people starting dates on the surface. Thirty days (Figuratively speaking) later once people break ground people find out they're not compatible.

In a nutshell, compatibility is about whether or not the multiple levels that makes up an individual are acceptable with another person. Acceptable sounds like such a strong word right? Similarities are important, but the differences are important too. Personally, I wouldn't want to be with a woman that is exactly like me. I would rather be in a balanced relationship where we have similarities and differences. Being in a relationship is about connecting and growing. That will not happen if two people do not pay attention to the differences too; however, it depends on which differences. I'm referring to differences as in strengths and weaknesses, specifically the weaknesses. I dated a woman named Chloe (Not her real name) not too long ago and she is an example of what I'm talking about. Chloe's strength was her ability to be compassionate and being able to express her compassion in ways that were always welcomed. My strength was in communication and trying to create an atmosphere in which open communication is always welcomed. Coincidently

(Purpose), my weakness was compassion and Chloe's was communication. It wasn't that I was not compassionate; it was how I communicated my compassion towards people.

When words left my mouth, I was thinking it was being compassionate, but those on the receiving end did not think so. Through being with Chloe, I've learned how to express compassion so the person on the other end knew it was compassion. Chloe has told me in the past, that she has learned about how important it is to communicate. In a sense the relationship with Chloe allowed for both of us to learn and grow through one another and to me that's what I like about life. Compatibility shouldn't just be focused on similarities, but also the differences and how the differences can be used for self-growth.

People run into problems when they have not learned about one of the levels of the other person during the "Dating Phase". Therefore, while they are in a "Relationship" with that person, he or she becomes shocked at was revealed. Dating isn't just about going on out with someone else. It's about learning about another person's life.

For example, asking about his or her day, observing how he or she handles situations, how he or she carries him or herself, etc. We learn about these examples by spending time around him or her, sharing experiences with him or her, listening to his or her experiences, and just plain ole- fashion conversation.

Nobody is going to know 111% about him or herself because we are constantly learning about life. Nor will anyone learn 111% about someone else; with that being said, we still must break ground on our individual foundations. I'm pretty sure there is someone right now saying, "Well, then how in the heck am I supposed to determine compatibility?" A lot of people use the "Pro vs. Con" for compatibility, but it's completely useless. For starters, sometimes what I do is break down human beings into parts to determine compatibility; I break myself down.

As human beings we are mental (intellectual & emotional), physical, and spiritual. When I go on a date with a woman I use four questions that are based on the four aspects above. I use what I know about me to fill in the four aspects. I refer to this method as "HB4.0"; however, you can call it what you want.

Ex.1 Human Beings	Maceo
Intellect	I love mental stimulation, conversations w/ depth, very curious mind.
Emotions	I address and embrace my emotions, I allow myself to feel, emotional integrity.
Physical	I live in the "Now" (I get into further details later in the chapters)
Spiritual	I believe all experiences (Positive & Negative) are to help us grow. Each experience has a lesson. Everlasting happiness is inside of all of us, not on the surface

Once I fill in the compatibility answers, I'm able to flip the answers into questions. They are simply a hit or miss. There is no negotiation on the compatibility questions. The reason for that is this is at my foundation. Remember, what is at your foundation never changes, no matter what happens on the surface (Externally).

Ex. 2 Human Beings	Maceo
Intellect	What are your observations of life?
Emotion	What do you define as emotional integrity? (I also observe women to see how they respond to their experiences; how and if they address their emotions)
Physical	Are you here?
Spiritual	What is your perception or observations of life? What's your definition of happiness?

I use this process for everything, especially when I reach a fork in the road. A Pro's vs. Con's list is too broad and never-ending. You can even use this for determining a career choice, etc.

Ex. 3 Human Beings	You
Intellect	Are analytical or critical thinking skills, etc needed for this career/job?
Emotion	Am I emotionally stable for what the career/job requires?
Physical	Do I have the physical resources for the career choice? From Internet access, PC, to equipment, etc. Am I physically fit for the position?
Spiritual	How will this career/job help me to grow and/or help other's to grow? Is creativity allowed and/or supported?

When we know what's at our foundations, we can use it to determine compatibility with someone else, which becomes especially useful when we are dating. Within one date, sometimes mid-way in the date, you can determine if the other person is compatible with your foundation. I have been on dates and knew within 8 minutes if a woman was compatible me. Utilizing the "HB4.0" method allows us from becoming less stressful or frustrated, down the road with finding out certain traits that are incompatible with our foundations.

Those who work in the construction field or new homeowners know that the foundation takes some time to build, and it's extremely important that its built with the right materials. Obviously, building with the right materials makes a lot of sense, since the whole house will be resting on the foundation. Here's a question, why can't we apply the same logic for building a house for building a relationship? Is it possible to do?

Sure it is, but before I continue you must rid your mind of the cloud of definitions set by society that you live by. The definitions of "What a man really wants/what is he thinking...what a woman really wants/what is she thinking etc."

The reason I said that statement is due to the fact that all men do not think a certain way nor do women. The fact that women point fingers at men and men point fingers at women proves that the problems are with our perceptions not the genders. "Society" has a big issue with being wrapped around the axle on the "Smaller

Pictures" compared to the "Big Pictures". Throughout the remainder of this book, you will see exactly what I'm talking about. So lets kick this off, shall we?

Chapter 2. Survey Foundation Site

It should be starting to resonate in your brain-housing group that a foundation is pertinent to building a relationship with someone else and oneself. In fact when was the last time you went on a date with yourself? Instead of gathering information from the outside world about what you should do in a relationship or how you should be acting; how about asking yourself. We have all the answers that we constantly search for. Ultimately, at the end of the day, you are the one who is in the relationship, not the outside world. Yes I said it, I know that may sound a bit odd since I'm technically a part of the outside world or am I?

There are tons of men and women who

want to have a relationship with someone else, but they don't have a relationship with themselves. Having a relationship with yourself is just as important. What is at the core of you are? Not as man or woman, but as an individual. The answers to this question will aid you in analyzing who is compatible with you. I'm not talking about things like what are your likes and dislikes; whether or not you are sweet and caring; you have to dig a little deeper than that. If we want to have a "Deep" relationship, then we must dig deep within ourselves.

Throughout this journey of life I have always had a different outlook on life, especially relationships. For one, I've learned how to healthily be alone, be content with myself, and enjoy life. You have to be able to love yourself. I know it sounds cheesy, but there are quite a few of people out there who do not love or respect themselves and actually expect others to do the same. Along my path of life, I've been learning so much from the various lessons of life and how important it is to redefine what life means to us, as individuals. So that entailed stepping back from society's "Norm", shifting my perspective, and re-approaching "Society's definitions." I've noticed that many of my definitions are not the same as everyone else's. I'm content with that, but I do often contemplate about life and wonder if people have redefined their lives. It seems like people are out of sync within themselves. Deep down people want one thing, but their actions express otherwise (I blame Society, not you). While being out of sync, they continue to chase what society says is the antidote; when the antidote has been inside all along.

Anyways, how many of you have been in a relationship with different definitions? Meaning you defined Love as...but the other individual defined it as... Letters create words; words create definitions; definitions create meanings; and meanings create expressions. Within our foundations are a plethora of definitions that guide our expressions on the surface. If you ever wondered why you act a certain way, turn inwards and survey your foundation site. On the other hand, if we are in relationships we should know what our own definitions are to be able to determine compatibility. Instead of following "Society's Definitions." I do not know if you notice, but everything "Society" says is bass-ackwards.

One of the statements that I hear quite frequently is, "I need me a woman or I need a man." A person does not need a man or woman in his or her lives in order to live a fulfilled life. According to Webster's Dictionary, a "Need" is defined by a physiological or psychological requirement for the well being of an organism. I'm just a bit confused, so I apologize for wasting your time, but I do have one question. When I hear women say "I need a man/bf/husband in my life to make me happy, feel special, etc"; they must actually need men to feel whole right? So by them stating that requirement, they are really saying that the essence of their life is and will be in the hands of the man whom she depends on for that necessity?

With all the focus being on "Needs", I wonder how many relationships actually "Share"? A relationship should be focused more on "Sharing" than "Needing" someone. One of the keywords in this sentence is sharing. There is a distinct difference between being a part of someone's life (Sharing) and someone being your life (Needing). The only healthy way to be a part of someone's life is to be able to stand by yourself prior to being in a relationship. It is not the "Independent" (own house and car) mindset that I'm referring to. On that note, there are two types of being "Independent". The first type is what I've observed from women with the "Independent" mindset of "I don't need a man for anything." Personally, I think that the women who have this mindset feel this way from being hurt so many times from a man. This type of "Independence" is stemming from emotional pain from depending on a man and the man coming up short. Every time I go on dates with these types of women they seem to only be concerned with proving to me that they do not need a man. Do you know how annoying that is? I remember one date with a woman who for some odd reason thought I cared about money. We met up at a restaurant and that is where the irritation began.

First, she said, "Look Maceo, I don't need no man for anything…Don't be reaching for your wallet after dinner cause I got this." That was strike one. When the waiter came around to start us off with some drinks she said, "Get any drink you want cause you know I'm paying". That was strike two. After we ordered drinks and were waiting for the waiter to return we started chit chatting. So I asked her one of my foundational questions, "What's your definition of happiness?" She said, "Anything that benefits me and getting that paper (money)." Strike three you're outta there; more like strike three I'm outta there. I told her, "Well, it's been a real pleasure and good luck with everything." She was like, "What you leaving? Why are you leaving?" "We are not compatible and since you stated several times that you were paying; you can go ahead and pick up the tab, later."

Having those foundational questions really save you from stress. The second type of "Independence" is completely the opposite of the example above. This type of independence is an action not a reaction (To being emotionally hurt).

A woman who realizes that she must be able to stand on her own her two feet and develop her self-relationship. A woman who is secure with herself first, knows how to healthily be alone, and still can enjoy life.

When I referred to "Standing" by yourself I meant to being able to: be healthily alone, be content with what's at your core, defining what happiness means to you, being able to address and embrace your emotions, etc. By "Standing" on our own, our observations of life and knowledge from experiences contribute to the foundation within us. The foundation is what equips us for our "Outward journey" and enables us to share our lives with another person. People will become able to share the multiple levels that encompass their individual lives; while maintaining their own lives and self-relationships.

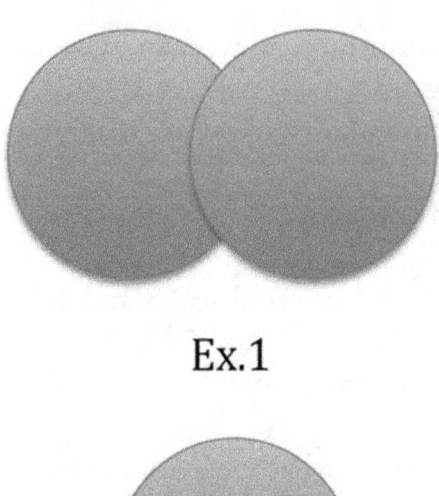

Ex.1

Ex.2

Example 1 represents two individuals who share their lives. When we share our lives there is still the "I" in our relationships. The "I" is not the "Ego-I"; the "I" refers to the identity. We still have our identities; we do not lose who we are as individuals or "Lose ourselves" in the relationship. We are still grounded in our individual lives and are able to follow our passions while sharing the multiple aspects of our being. In order to even share your life, you must have a foundation. Without the foundation, you're pretty much sharing what is on the surface which changes like the seasons change. When you connect at the foundation the connection will always be there no matter which seasons pass through.

Example 2 illustrates someone being your life. Have you noticed that there is no second circle? There is no second circle because you "Lost yourself" in being with your significant other. You have lost the "I" in the relationship; you lost who you were. Every choice, decision, thought, and action is geared towards your significant other. You live your life for your significant other and that is completely unhealthy. Some people believe that giving all of who they are is right. It is right; however, you're not supposed to lose yourself in the process. People can still give all of who they are by opening up every aspect of their lives and allowing another individual to share the different aspects of his or her lives.

If I lost you, hopefully this helps: picture a skyscraper with walkways on multiple levels that stretch across to the other skyscraper. When someone is your life, you have decided to abandon your individual foundation and hop on someone else's. So what you end up with, is a relationship with no foundation and these types of relationships do more harm than good. When this type of relationship does fail, you feel like crap. You cannot make sense of the failed relationship because you believe you gave everything; you gave yourself for the relationship. Then you start to say to yourself, "Why can't I find a good man" or "Why can't I find a good woman".

Additionally, example 2 represents someone who is not grounded in his or her own life. Meaning if you are not grounded in your life and you're just "floating", then it becomes extremely easy to lose yourself in a relationship. We have to have a balance in every aspect of our lives and relationships are no different. When two individuals share they're balancing his or her individual lives and his or her relationship. On the other hand, when an individual is "Someone's life" there is no balance because there is no identity; he or she lost who they were. Make Sense?

Anyways, It really frustrates me that too many people (Men & Women of all ages, sexual orientations, nationalities, etc) actually think that they "Need someone" in their lives to make them happy or feel special (I do not blame you, I blame Society). I know of six relationships right off the top of my head, including marriages, which were built on "Needing one another".

Of those, I know of four that have ended due to the "Needs" not being met. This has been said to you or you know someone that it was said to, "I cheated on you because you didn't make any time for me or showed me attention etc". Guess what? I can guarantee that the person that said those words most likely NEEDED a relationship, with someone who would show them attention.

Now, I am not some person who is writing out of pain and unresolved emotions that still need to be addressed, or someone who has shielded his heart because of it being broken too many times. I am the person who realizes that in order to exist, I need myself because without me, I am nothing; I do not exist. So for someone to think he or she "Needs" someone is to say he or she is nothing; they do not exist-without having someone in their lives to complete that "Need". So I ask you...what do you need from a man or woman?

I used to be on a social networking site that also had a chat room feature. There were various chat rooms for different: locations, nationalities, sports, music, etc. The chatrooms were very unique; in the sports chatroom you could come across someone with a foot fetish, which I thought was quite humorous. The thing about the chat rooms that I thought was intriguing was the freedom of speech. There was one particular woman that caught my eye, who kept posting the same post: "Looking for a jealous man, needs him to be very controlling, and wants a serious relationship."

At first glance I thought this woman was out of her mind, but when I thought about it some more I realized she wasn't. Now, why would anyone want to be in a relationship with a jealous person? That was the first question that popped into my head; the second one was, "What does someone do when they are jealous?" The jealous person becomes more concerned with the whereabouts of his or her significant other. He or she wants the significant other to be around him or her more often. He or she doesn't want the significant other out with anyone new or anyone at all. The reason I believe this particular woman would want that kind of relationship is to have someone who will: show her attention, make her feel special, make her feel needed.

Like I previously stated, she wasn't out of her mind, she just modified the qualities of a man in order to get what she needed. However, she gets what she "needs" at the expense of an unhealthy relationship. Most likely the "Non-jealous" men from her previous relationships did not: show her attention, make her feel special or needed. This is an example of how we can easily look outwards and make some changes (unhealthy ones), when it's the inside-of-us that needs to change.

Within the chat rooms I would always see post from men and women of who they were and what they were or were not looking for. For example: 18 male I need a girlfriend, 44 male looking for a serious relationship, 35 female I need a REAL Man that knows how to treat a woman, 26 male looking for REAL Love, 62 female divorced looking for man that doesn't lie or cheat, 18 female looking for a man that shows me attention. The ages, genders or sexual orientations are completely irrelevant but what is relevant is what they're looking for isn't quite right.

We must come to an understanding that boyfriends, girlfriends, and "Serious relationships" do not happened over night (Unless you're in Vegas). The reason for that is relationships are built (Just like houses); boyfriends, girlfriends, fiancée's happen during the building process. For some odd reason people want to leap from the grass, straight up to the first floor expecting things to just "Pick up".

In other words people haven't built their own individual foundation nor established a connection to someone else's. Then they rush right in to being someone's boyfriend/girlfriend, and when it fails so quickly, they wonder why. It fails due to no foundation between the two people; without a foundation there is no first floor (Boyfriend/girlfriend).

Without a first floor there is no second floor (Husband/Wife). In order to have access to the first floor and eventually the second floor there needs to be a foundation; two individual foundations equal one-strong foundation.

In a healthy relationship, two people contribute to building the foundation. If one person is the only person building there is no way a relationship will rest on its uneven foundation. There isn't any easy way around it; if we want a healthy relationship we have to build. This is equivalent to someone running a marathon. People want to cross the finish line and say "I'm a long distance runner; a marathon finisher". But the people do not want to train their selves in order to prepare themselves for running 26.2 miles; a marathon; a long distance run. People want to find a way to not run the full 26.2 miles, and still be able to cross the finish line as a marathon finisher. This analogy correlates to those who want a long-term relationship, but haven't prepared him or her selves.

If we want a serious relationship, we must be serious with ourselves first. Be serious about building our own individual foundations. We need to be true and real to ourselves. I get so tired of hearing "I keep it a hundred"; meaning one hundred percent real, when it's really one hundred percent fake. If we want something real we must be real. We shouldn't have to change, act a different way, or modify who we are just to get in a relationship. If we do how is that being real? Then there are people thinking that it's the Man's fault or it's the Woman's fault for why we cannot find a healthy relationship. It's neither the man's nor the woman's fault; it's the individual's fault. Now that's one hundred percent real!

We live in a society where it's always the other person's fault for why we can't do or have anything in life. It's easier for people to point fingers at other people; it's hard for us to turn that finger and point it at ourselves. The question is why? We heard the saying before, "The truth hurts". Well, let it hurt and allow yourself to feel and stop telling yourself lies. Think about it, if we tell ourselves one lie, then we end up telling ourselves another lie to cover up that lie and the cycle continues. We get to a point where our true selves are tangled and buried beneath lies. Then we have the nerve to say, "I hate being lied to or why can't men or women be honest with me?"

Everything in life starts with us.

What exactly is a serious relationship? That's a really good question, one that I'll attempt to take a stab at. I think it's a relationship that's built on a solid foundation in which two people are connected beneath the surface, while continuing to grow on multiple levels in their lives. Once again, that's my simplified definition, what's your definition?

I've noticed that people assume that everyone should know what "Treat me good" means. What one persons definition of "Treat me good" may be entirely different to someone else. We assume that common sense would prevail; however, people should be able to use definitions to explain what they're referring to. In the past I briefly dated one woman who believed that "Treat me good", meant that I was supposed to be her private ATM and when she "rang", I was supposed to "hop to".

Another woman I dated told me, "If you have to ask what treat me good means, then you don't know how to treat a woman." She was definitely accurate with that answer and that was probably the only similarity that we shared. Not all women are the same, meaning what would be considered 'great' for one woman, could be the complete opposite for another. So, instead of looking for something with interchangeable definitions, how about specifying on the qualities that one is compatible with.

The number one posts in the chat rooms that people were looking for was REAL/TRUE Love. I'd sure like to know what's the difference between "Love and REAL/TRUE Love or Man vs. REAL Man, for that matter. Everything starts with us, we may have influences of what love is, etc., but we still must be able to make sense of what love means to us as individuals, not "Man" or "Woman".

Up to this point, I've given my definition to every subject matter that I posed a question on. Love to me, falls under the category in life that cannot be articulated into words. The closest way to describe it, it's like a feeling but not an emotion. It's not a physical pain or ache; it's like an intense powerful feeling between our emotions and our physical body. A feeling that is felt no matter the physical distance between two people; although, the closer a person is to the other, the stronger and more profound the feeling becomes.

The feeling is felt even when words are not spoken. Love is a connection like how we feel connected to music without lyrics; the music comforts our spirit.

While being in Love with someone we still continue to learn about life, as individuals and through the one's we love. The learning does not stop when we enter love; it just brings two people closer to the point that he or she becomes one in life. When we become that close, there really is not anything that two people cannot tackle together. When love enters a relationship it does not mean people will never have arguments or disagreements. Love is what enables two people to openly communicate; love is what allows humility over pride; love is what allows compassion over apathy.

I believe there is a part inside of all us that cannot be rationalized or put inside a box. When we put things in a box, we attempt to control it and our rational minds try to solve it. But, the rational side of us cannot even approach it. We try our hardest to explain, but sometimes there are not enough words in the human language to express the feelings that we experience. This is the place that I believe love is; love is outside the box.

I was on a date with a woman not too long ago and we were talking about relationships. Kim (Not her real name) was telling me how she had been hurt a lot and wondered if there were any decent men left. So I asked her "Can you define decent?" Kim said "A man that's a gentleman who will love me and is ready to settle down with me. I cater to my man; I cook, clean, and I have the biggest heart. I'm tired of being cheated on and used." So then I said "Tell me about yourself." "I'm sweet, caring, honest, mature an all around fun person, and I'm drama free." Then I said, "That's nice. What's beneath the surface? I want to know about who you are as an individual. What's at your core?" Then Kim I said "Can you just ask me questions and get to know me?" I said, "I am trying to get to know you."

The 'tell me about yourself' statement is very common when we're on dates with other people. The issue with the answer that Kim gave me was the fact that it was universal. I'm sweet, caring, honest, etc, so does that mean that we were compatible? Maybe, but the answer is once again right on the surface. Think about it like this, I can randomly choose four women that could give me the same answer that Kim gave me. The point is, what is beneath the surface that separates Kim from the other randomly chosen women? Beneath the surface is the place that I wanted to learn about Kim, and that's the place that Kim should want to learn about Kim too. Beneath the surface at the foundation, is what makes every individual unique; what separates him or her from everyone else.

The questions that Kim wanted to hear, were the questions that most people ask: What kind of music do you listen to, are you religious, are you working, do you have any goals, what do you do for a living, etc? The answers to these questions vary in importance from one person to the next; but if we do not connect beneath the surface then these answers are irrelevant. People run into problems when they are on dates and ask these types of questions. Then down the road, people learn about what's beneath the surface, and they realize they aren't compatible with them. That's when people begin to say "Next time I meet someone they must be..." This is why I start off each date with "Foundation Questions", and they can only be used because I know what's at my foundation.

Chapter 3. Construction Failures

Sometimes the thought of past experiences frighten us from even addressing them. They've caused so much pain and agony that facing them head on stirs emotions that we really prefer not to be bothered with. But when you think about it, those are the experiences that bring so much meaning to our lives in the present.

Our experiences are a part of what makes us who we are today. We cannot just address the positive experiences and glorify how much we learned from them, and bury the negative experiences in a filing cabinet. Life has so much more to offer us but our unhealthy relationships (The types are irrelevant) are consuming our lives. Some people are holding on to burdens that are hindering their growth as well as not allowing them to enjoy life.

Leah (Not her real name) was a woman that I dated when I was in the Marine Corps. When I look back on our relationship, it was definitely a "Surface" relationship; however, that relationship had a lot of lessons in store for me. It wasn't until recently that I realized it was our relationship that started one continuous learning lesson.

It was early in the economic meltdown several years ago; I was just relieved from duty in the barracks on base. My cell phone rang, "Hello" I said. For the first few seconds all I heard was crying on the other end then Leah said quickly, "I just got laid off from my main job". Leah worked one full time job and worked part time at another. I replied, "Slow down, what do you mean you got laid off; you've been at that job longer than anyone else." She said, "I just got to work today and was notified." Then I said, "Don't worry too much about it, you can use this to your advantage. Get yourself together and put together a resume. I'll look on base to see if there are any available positions that fit your work experience." So Leah said, "But what am I going to do?" I replied, "Get your resume together and see if you can pick up more hours at your other job. I got a formation to get to and then I'm secured for the weekend. I'll talk to you afterwards. Don't stress yourself too much." She said, "Okay, I'll talk to you later."

    I knew losing her job was unfortunate, since it was her primary source of income and she enjoyed her job. On the other hand, she had previously told me that she wanted to go into law enforcement. So my response was based on thinking that she could now use the additional time to prepare mentally and physically for the police academy, while working at her other job. Also the fact that she had a lot of experience at the job (where she was laid off), made me think maybe she could possibly find work on base. One of the keywords here is "Thinking", I should have been feeling.

Sunday rolled around and I invited Leah over. So I had to pick her up outside of the gate and bring her on base. When she got in my car, I noticed she looked either angry or down, I couldn't figure it out. So I said, "Are you still bothered about the job situation?" Leah said, "Bothered isn't the word that I would classify it as Maceo." She said, "We can discuss it when we get to your room". I said to myself, "Oh gosh, this night is not going how I played it out in my head." While I was driving I started to do what anyone would do in my shoes; I started reviewing everything I said to her the day she lost her job. "I was caring and tried to help the situation, maybe she isn't mad at me." So I looked at her face and said to myself, "Oh yeah she is tight lipped; she's mad.

Usually she holds my hand while I drive, not this time; her hands her folded." So we get to barracks and walk to my room. Leah sits down on the bed; I pulled up a chair, and asked her, "What's wrong with you?" She said, "I've been thinking about what you said to me the other day when I called you about my job." I said, "Okay and..." She said, "Don't cut me off, I'm not another Marine, you shouldn't have talked to me like that." "Leah being Marine has nothing at all to do with what I said. I figured you could use the loss of your job to your advantage, since you said that you wanted to become a police officer. I was thinking you could use the new time you have to prepare yourself for the academy. I was pretty much thinking down the road, how this experience can help you."

Then she said, "That's the thing Maceo, I need you to be there for me, you don't always need to say something. Just be there and listen."Leah and I used to keep in touch but lost contact over time. Our relationship was the first lesson for me in learning to be compassionate. Which I find ironic because my mom used to say to me "You need to be more compassionate, women like men that are compassionate." It took me to date a few more women after Leah before the "Light bulb" when it off.

There are times when we cannot comprehend our experiences or we get frustrated with going through the same experiences. For example, have you ever noticed that the last few people you were in a relationship with were identical? Regardless of their nationality, age, employment status, etc, you felt like you were dating the same person each time. This is the ideal time to change our perspective of that experience. Sometimes the same experience continues to happen over and over again because we failed to learn from it. In other words, sometimes we end up "Dating the same people" because we didn't learn what we should have learned the first time.

Within each one of our experiences is a learning lesson, which can be missed if our perception is on the surface.

There are two aspects of learning when learning pertains to relationships. The first aspect is always connected with the emotional component of us; how emotionally involved we are with the other person. Especially when we are emotionally bogged down from dating someone or being in an unhealthy relationship with them. The majority of us choose this aspect of learning, due to the emotional reactions to an experience. For instance, if we are in a relationship with someone and we find out that he or she is cheating on us, we feel hurt by it.

Eventually when we recover from our broken heart, we ask ourselves "What did I learn from this"? Our answer to this question is connected to the emotional response from finding out we were cheated on. The answers are usually along the lines of: "I've learned to never date another man/woman that lies, I'm never dating anyone who is like this person, I'm not giving my heart to anyone again, I learned that I have to protect my heart better, etc."

The second aspect of learning is when we shift our perspective on the experience. We shift our perspective to the point where we can address the emotions while analyzing the experience. Staying with the example of cheating, this aspect of learning poses these questions: "What caused him/her to cheat, what did I not do to cause him/her to cheat, what did I learn about myself from him/her cheating?" Now, these questions may have been used with the first aspect of learning, but the analysis and lessons learned from the questions is what makes this aspect of learning so profound.

Common Reasons/Excuses for Cheating:

-Being bored in the relationship/no excitement

-Physically Attracted to someone else

-Significant other not showing the other person attention/feel special

- Significant other doesn't make the other person happy

-Significant other works too much/workaholic

-Under the influence of alcohol and/or drugs

It does not matter who cheats, there is always a reason why the person decided to cheat and most likely its on that list above. He or she cheating and how its unbelievable shouldn't be the main focus. If we were lucky enough to know the reason why they cheated, then we can focus on the "Why's". Even if we did not know the reason why he or she cheated, we can still put the puzzle together.

Boredom

Most healthy relationships usually arrive at a place where it feels like a 9to5 job Monday through Friday. The excitement and pursuit during the early stages have worn out, and the relationship has become boring. That's why communication is imperative in any relationship. Several years ago I was in a relationship with a woman where boredom snuck in. I started to notice the initial excitement of seeing my girlfriend and going on dates with her, started to fade away. So what did I do? I talked to her about my observations. Which I'm glad I did because she felt the same way too. So we talked about ways to freshen up our relationship. The both of us had an adventurous side, so we decided to put that side to use. Instead of following the same routine of dates, we chose to go hiking one day. We had so much fun, exploring and creating new memories that we planned to go on an adventure once a month. With a little communication and creativity, boredom never snuck in again.

On the opposite end of the spectrum, are those who are bored and decide to cheat. What's the connection between boredom and cheating? Failure to communicate is what surfaces to my mind. If you're bored in a relationship, all you have to do is communicate it to the other person. It really is that simple. If you care and value the relationship, then you would want to find a way to improve it. Those that do not care or value the relationship, cheat. The other question to ask is "Why was he or she bored in the relationship"? To be bored is to have a loss of interest, in this case, a loss of interest in the relationship. Here is another question, "What did he or she find interesting about me to want to be in a relationship in the first place?" There had to be a reason why he or she wanted to be in a relationship and that reason may be linked to why he or she was bored.

Learning Lesson: When the interests are shallow, people run into boredom and cheat. But when the interests have some depth people communicate what they feel, want to improve the relationship and do not cheat. Meaning when the interests for the relationship are on the surface (opposite of foundation), there is nothing that grounds the person from deciding to cheat. When there is that deeper connection between two people, then cheating doesn't even enter the thought process.

Physical Attraction

There are some beautiful people on this place that we call Earth, just because we are in a relationship doesn't mean that we will not find others attractive. When I was in relationships with other women, I always came across beautiful women. However, that physical attraction wasn't enough for me to want to end my relationship or to cheat on my current girlfriend. It did not matter if I was in a relationship for one month or one year.

The types of people that cheat in a relationship, due to being physically attracted to someone else, did not build his or her relationship on solid ground. Meaning, if physical attraction pulls someone from a relationship, then the relationship didn't have a strong foundation or none at all.

Learning Lesson: When you're dating someone the conversation should have more depth, than just how physically attractive you are to the other person. If two people decided to be in a relationship with each other based on attraction alone, then it's only a matter of time before someone cheats. You can tell during your dates, if the person is compatible with your foundation. How? By asking "Foundation Questions" which are questions based on what is at your foundation.

Not Showing The Other Attention

This is when the benefit from developing a self- relationship comes to light. When we know how to healthily be alone and enjoy our own company, we learn how to show ourselves attention. Technically, we are not alone when we have a relationship with self. Forget about what others say about you and how you "need" someone.

We can still live and enjoy our lives. When we enter a relationship with someone else, we will know how to show ourselves attention. So we will not depend on the other individual to give us attention and we can focus on building a strong foundation with the right materials. You cannot build a strong foundation based on the other person showing you attention.

Those that cheat due to their significant other not showing them attention, is from not having a self-relationship. Meaning instead of choosing to turn inwards he or she turned outwards, towards another person. If that person had been able to show him or herself attention, there would be no need to "Step outside the boundaries of the relationship."

These types of people usually have a few insecurities and depend on the other person to make them feel special. Once again a relationship is about sharing, not needing. They believe it is the other person's duty to make them feel special and when his or her need isn't met, he or she cheats! Logically speaking, because of these people's mindset, cheating isn't wrong. By someone not showing him or her attention, he or she may have trouble figuring out if the other person is still interested. Meaning he or she always used "Attention" to determine if someone is still interested in him or her.

Learning Lesson: You avoid these types of people by observing them when you're dating them. Usually these types of people need for you to make contact with them every waking minute throughout the day. Whether it's through: text messaging, phone calls, web cams, etc. And of course they expect and look forward to seeing your "Good Morning" text message when they wake up. In his or her minds, if you don't contact them throughout the day, that means you're not interested.

Now try not to get wrapped around the axle;

meaning, when we are interested in someone we want to show them that they are on our minds. But these people are "Attention seekers"; they 'need' this to feel special.

Not Making the Other Person Happy

For some odd reason we live in a society in which people believe that it is their significant other's responsibility to make him or her happy. You probably heard this before, "I'm looking for a man to make me happy" or "I'm looking for a woman to make me happy." I personally believe that two individuals should be individually happy prior to being in a relationship.

Once again when two individuals have happiness beneath the surface he or she is able to share happiness, instead of depending on someone to make him or her happy. If a person depends on a significant other and he or she fails, then a person will cheat. The "Cheater" will find another person who can 'make him or her happy'.

Learning Lesson: When dating a person you should be able to determine if her or she has happiness in his or her life. Specifically, a person should have internal happiness, which can only be found beneath the surface. Internal happiness is constantly flowing through one's life and nothing externally can change it.

External happiness is always sought after, but only provides "Temporary happiness". Anyone who has ever dated someone with external happiness, knows that this happiness changes just as much as the weather does. By knowing your individual foundation and knowing your internal happiness you can develop questions to aid in compatibility. I get further into happiness in the "Foundation of Happiness" chapter.

Significant other is a workaholic

Nowadays it seems like people are even more stressed out. Particularly, stress from finances or relationships and some people rolled snake eyes. They leave from their main job stressed out; to go to their second job, then arrive home to be further stressed out by their significant other. What does the significant other have to say, "You're always working" or "I don't even see you in the mornings".

That's if you're lucky; if your significant other does not live with you, then it's even worse. Those of us who support ourselves financially will not deny overtime just so we can spend time with our significant others, especially the way this economy is right now. I know that may sound cold hearted but look at it like this: work overtime, pay bills, and reschedule. Compared to deny overtime, possible eviction/credit score plunges, and spending a romantic evening with our significant other. The whole time we spend with our significant other we are thinking of ways to supplement our income or "Pick up the slack". The former sounds a bit more comforting to me. Would you choose the former or the latter?

Also there are a few people out there who are confused in relationships when it comes down to working/careers. Remember relationships are about sharing. Sharing originates when we develop connections with another person beneath the surface. However, people still have their individual lives; meaning, they still have hobbies and careers/jobs. People for some reason really believe that a person should abandon his or her career/job for the relationship. Of course this is romantic and could give us a bunch of "Warm fuzzies" inside; however, warm fuzzies do not pay the rent or mortgage. A person who cheats because of his or her significant other being a workaholic; really comes down to the significant other not showing him or her enough attention. So he or she blames the significant other for choosing work over attention.

After I got out of the Marines, I went back to college as a full-time student. The Veteran benefits (POST 9/11 GI Bill) included having our tuition 100% paid for and also providing Veterans will a living allowance (BAH) based on our credit hours. So pretty much I was getting paid to go to college; college was my new job. When I met women one of the first things I told them was that I'm in college and my classes are my number one priority. Several times I chose to be on a date with my political science textbook in the library than with a woman. What I found sort of funny was how the women were supportive when I told them my classes were priority one. Nevertheless, when it came down to them wanting to hangout with me and me saying I was hanging out in the library they were not supportive anymore. There was one particular woman who stood out compared to the other women I dated while I was in college.

Marie (Not her real name) went to another college in the area and we met at a sports bar. She loved football (NFL) and actually watched the games, which I thought was very cool. I rarely meet women who actually care about the calls that referees make in football games. Anyways, we exchanged numbers and got together the following weekend for some sushi. I told her that I was in college majoring in Political Science and she said she was majoring in Business Administration.

We continued to date and see each other when our schedules allowed it. When I got my midterm grades, I noticed I was not doing as well as should have been doing. So I told myself, "I need to spend more time in the library than with Marie." I called Marie and told her, "Just got my midterm grades, we're going to have to tone down the amount of time we see each other." Marie said, "I totally understand Maceo." So approximately four days passed by and I get a text message from Marie, "Hey, I haven't seen u in awhile want to go to the movies?" I replied, "No I'm studying in the library, I'll ttyl after I'm done. About four hours passed by and I get another text, "Hey babe ru still studying?" "Yes I am", I replied. "Ok txt/call me when ur done." So when I was done at the library, I sent her a text saying I was done and headed home.

When I got home I grabbed me something to eat, took a shower, then hit the bed. I woke up to six text messages from Marie and four missed calls. The first text message said, "Ru still busy, when ru going to make some time for me" and the second text message said, "Hey why ru ignoring me?" The four remaining text messages were all question marks.

The first thought that crossed my mind when I read those text messages was, "Are you freaking kidding me; she just doesn't get it." So I sent her a text, "No I'm not ignoring you, I was sleep when you sent those messages. I thought you understood that I needed to focus on my studies." Marie replied, "Look I need a man that cares about me more than anything else. You don't care about spending time with me. I'm the only one trying to spend time with you. Delete my number, Bye." I said to myself, "Is she serious?" I know this example did not end with me being cheated on, but I wanted to give an example of how working/college student can be an issue with someone who craves attention.

Learning Lesson: When you are out on dates make sure you articulate what you do for a living. I've noticed that when people do not have a career/job and they are dating someone who does, they become the person who despises the other person working. I think if people are in a surface-based relationship and someone does not work or have something he or she is working towards, they are more inclined to cheat.

Under The Influence of Alcohol and/or Drugs

Some of us may enjoy alcohol beverages with friends, family, and our significant others at social gatherings. Anyone that knows me, especially those that I served with in the Marines, knows that I enjoy partaking an alcohol beverages. I do not think there is a problem with consuming alcohol as long as the individuals are in control of his or her actions. While under the influence of alcohol, I have never bent or broke the law. Nor has breaking the law ever crossed my mind or cheating. Without alcohol my sense of humor and ability to make others laugh is out of this world, so with alcohol my sense of humor just intensifies and I become even funnier.

Then there are people that consume alcohol/drugs and once again decide to cheat. You have probably heard something along these lines: "Come on now, I was drunk that's why I cheated" or "You know I love you, but the alcohol and/or drugs took over" or "It was the alcohol and/or drugs, not the real me." Regardless of the reasons why the individual/s cheated there were probably a few red flags that you missed.

Learning Lesson: When there is a drastic shift in a person's personality and behavior when consuming alcohol you may want to become more observant. The ability to observe your significant other plays a critical role. Not just observing your significant other when you all are under the influence, but also when there is no alcohol in the picture. If your significant other breaks or bends the law without being under the influence of alcohol and/or drugs, then do you really think he or she will not bend or break the confines of a relationship? Even worse, if he or she is under the influence while bending or breaking the law, do you really believe that he or she will not cheat on you? If someone cannot abide by the laws in his or her own life, then how can he or she respect the confines of a relationship?

If you and your significant other are on dates without alcohol and he or she flirts with every man or woman then that's a red flag. With alcohol, it's only a matter of time before that "Friendly" conversation leads to a friendly conversation with tongue. In conversations about relationships the word, "morals" is always present. I can tell you this a person who has morals will still have morals with or without alcohol. If a person consumes alcohol and morals goes out the window, then there were no morals to begin with. Having morals is not a part-time way of life it's either full-time or none at all.

When I first started dating Christina not too long ago, we dated on and off for about a year or so. While we were talking on the phone one day she let me know something about her and alcohol. Christina said, "Sometimes when I drink I kiss or make-out with other women." I replied with a simple, "Okay, thanks for letting me know that." I respected the fact that she had enough integrity to let me know. However, I'm not the type of guy that's okay with dating a woman that makes out with other women when she's intoxicated. When I told my buddies about it, they thought I was crazy for losing interest in her. I knew that Christina and I just started dating, but hearing that made me lose interest.

Think about it like this, If I "Opened the gate" for that behavior, "Where could I possibly draw the line?" Would there even be a line anymore? Hypothetically speaking, I wonder how

Christina would have reacted if I told her that I make-out with other women when I consume alcohol. Would Christina be okay with going out for drinks and seeing me make out with another woman or several women? Of course she wouldn't be okay it. If she is not okay with that, then how could she possibly think I'd be okay with it?

Chapter 4. Framework

Understanding what our emotions are and where they stem from, can aid us with learning from our experiences. By asking yourself those basic question-words that we all learned as a child: who, what, when, where, why, and how will help us reach an understanding of our emotions. There is nothing wrong with being emotional, but there is a problem when we do not address and control our emotions or allow ourselves to feel.

Addressing your emotions is as simple as embracing them and understanding why you feel a certain way. When I talk about control, I'm not talking about not allowing yourself to feel. I'm talking about not letting your emotions cloud your perception. That's why it's not smart to make decisions when we're in an emotionally unstable state and we haven't addressed our emotions.

Emotions are a part of who we are as human beings, and when we do not address them they will cause a domino effect of catastrophes in our lives whether we're consciously aware or not. Men and women are human beings, so men and women are emotional. Of course there are different ways to express our emotions and that varies from person to person. Notice that I stated person to person and not from man to woman. According to "Society" men aren't emotional and if they show emotion then they aren't men. Hold up a second, isn't anger an emotion? So men can get angry but not emotional? That sure makes a lot of sense. What I find interesting is our DNA.

A male's is XY and a female's is XX and yet "Society" says, "Men and Women are wired so differently." Once again, I'm not a college graduate but isn't the X-chromosome from the mother?

Isn't the X-chromosome the common link between a male and a female? It's not that Men and Women are wired differently; some of them just need to hop outside the box and wake up. Well, if I allow society to dictate how I live my life, then I'm in no way shape or form a man. I'm not a man because I choose to communicate instead of bottling up my emotions. I'm not a man because I face my emotions head on and stare them right in the eye. I'm not a man because I could care less about how much money a woman makes. On that note, when I date women

I'm interested in who they are as individuals; I'm not dating their salaries. I'm not a man because I can date a woman in a so-called "Man's Profession", for instance like a woman who is a mechanic. I'm not a man because I watch and own romance movies aka "Chick Flicks". And the biggest of them all, I'm not a man because I'm not afraid to cry. In fact, I had a good cry earlier today, and it felt great!

According to "Patriarchal Society", crying is a show of weakness for men. How exactly is that so? I comprehend that all human beings are emotional and men and women are human beings; thus, men and women are emotional. Just like usual, "Society" has it bass-ackwards, I think crying is a show of strength. Men who do not allow themselves to cry because of what society says, are ignorant. By definition, ignorant means without education and/or knowledge. So they probably didn't receive the memo on humans being emotional. The human body is a fascinating creation. I think when we cry, the tears act like some sort of signal that lets us (Men & Women) know that we can pick up the other person's energy. In a way, by crying we are allowing ourselves to feel and I think that's where the strength comes from. Allowing our bodies freedom to do what it feels like doing.

On the contrary, when we do not allow our bodies to cry, how is that being strong? To me, that's a show of weakness. Weakness in the sense that "Men" cannot embrace their tears because of living their lives for "Society". In other words "Men" that live their lives based on what others say about them; that doesn't show strength that shows intimidation, which is the opposite of strength. Once again, "Society" is "Bass-Ackwards". Again try not to get wrapped around the axle. I'm not stating that the strength of a man is defined by shedding tears; I'm stating that "Society" is wrong in the belief of crying meaning a man is not strong.

Personally, I do not think there is a definition for being a Man. I believe I'm a "Man" based on evolution from being a newborn baby boy to being an adult male. I cannot define what a "Man" is and neither can anyone else. But people can ask me about who I am as an individual or who I am as Maceo M. NeSmith III. Society has many issues with trying to put everything in a box and "Labeling" it. We cannot put a definition of a man or a woman in a box because of individuals being outside the box. What's your definition of a "Man"? What's your definition of a "Woman"?

Have you ever laughed so hard that you started crying? Those are the best laughs, by contracting your abs when you laugh that hard, you can leave from a joke with a six-pack. Why is it accepted to cry from laughing but not from hurt feelings? Ever notice how we have open communication during laughter, but when our feelings are hurt the communication window closes?

Whenever we laugh to ourselves or around others it's because of finding something funny. Sometimes others around us will find it funny too, so they laugh along. Then there are those times that we laugh at something and someone doesn't understand why, so we tell him or her the reason. For some odd reason when our feelings are hurt some of us shut down and do not want to communicate our feelings to others. Our communication door closes and our feelings are trapped inside.

We all have reasons for clamming up at one point or another; what it usually comes down to is fear. We fear being judged from how others may react to what we are feeling. Even worse, we fear the judgment that we may cast on ourselves. No one wants to be that person who puts his or her feelings out in the open and the door to the other person slams shut. We fear feeling familiar emotions that may trigger past emotions or experiences.

In the past we might have been sad or

depressed and we don't ever want to feel that way again. So we end up labeling ourselves based on the feelings of being sad or depressed; we judge ourselves. So we clam up and close up shop because we think if we don't face them, then we don't have to worry about them. Or we shrug off the hurt feelings and "Keep it moving", as if nothing ever happened. We think this works but it doesn't happen like that. Ultimately, we end up internalizing the unaddressed feelings and start to form our own personal snowflake. You heard of the snowball effect right?

Each time we hold on to our feelings we are really adding more snowflakes to the one we already have. Until one day something "Sets us off", and out comes an avalanche. This avalanche is full of every hurt feeling we have ever held on to. Here's a question, why does it take an avalanche for us to convey how we feel?

Instead we could have conveyed how we felt and released the snowflake. You may think "I'm only human"; yes you are, but we still have to address our emotions. As humans we have the gift to feel and with any gift we have responsibilities. The fact of the matter is if we expect someone else to have emotional integrity, then we must have it too.

You probably wonder how I went from communication to emotional integrity right? Emotional integrity is the ability for an individual to openly express what he or she is feeling. What I cannot understand is how people cannot be honest with themselves about their own feelings. It's your feelings if there is anyone that should be able to understand them it's you. Inside ourselves is where we should be the most secure. Some of us may feel that we have a certain image that we must uphold, and addressing our emotions would conflict with that image. Our emotions are a part of our image; at least it is when you look from the inside out. When you're on the inside looking out all you have is you. I think the question I should ask is why do you care about what others 'think' about "Your image"? When you are the one who has to deal with the 'feelings'.

When we are in a relationship with someone else and an issue arises, we want to get to the bottom of the issue right? We can take a complex situation and break it down until we get a simplified answer. The same way we worked through complex mathematical problems with multiple variables during our years in academia. The same concept applies with addressing our emotions. That's the beauty of life any concept we learn is transferable to any aspect of life. You do not need a Ph. D in psychology to understand your own emotions, your life experiences is your Ph. D. You do not need a Ph. D in sociology to understand the problems around you; your observation of life is your Ph.D.

When we are faced with an experience that stirs our emotions all we have to do is relax and break down our emotions, the same way we break down mathematical problems. We break it down using our curious mind and those analytical skills that we all possess. If you're curious if you have analytical skills ask yourself this, "Have I ever asked a Why-question?" Of course you have, all of us have asked at least one why-question in our lives.

We can use our rational mind to analyze our emotions. It's like we have our own personal checks and balance's system within us. It's fairly simple, all you have to do is ask yourself questions (Who, what, when, where, why and how) about your emotions and be honest when you answer the questions. People usually have problems with the honesty part. There is no easy way around it, you have to be honest with yourself. If you do not like the answers at least you know how YOU really feel. It is pretty simple when you think about it. Do you have emotional integrity?

I cannot understand how we can trust someone else to confide in outside of us and talk about our emotions to him or her, but cannot do it with him or herself. Think about it like this:

Ex.1 Say you go to a restaurant to get some food. You receive a menu from the waiter and began to browse the menu to look for something good to eat. You stop at an entrée but notice that the dish has ingredients that do not agree with your digestive system. When the waiter comes back to your table, you order the entrée, but tell the waiter to not include certain ingredients.

Ex. 2 Say there are some issues in your relationship and you decide to confide in someone about the problems. You tell that certain person the issues and articulate your thoughts and feelings to him or her. This person is just like the waiter; he or she is on the receiving-end of the conversation.

The "Big picture" of these examples is that people have the ability to articulate their thoughts and feelings, even when the person on the opposite end is just listening. The same way we articulate our thoughts and feelings on the outside, is the same way we can do it on the inside. I know the two examples may sound like they are from "Left field", but there is some truth if you can shift your perspective. Try not to get wrapped around the axle on one example being about food and the other being about issues in relationships. The concept is articulation and that's what matters. Insecurities which take root on the inside are worked out on the inside not the outside. If insecurities are not worked on the inside, they will continue to grow and nothing on the outside will change them. Which is probably why people still feel insecure when they change things externally. Everything starts with us, as individuals.

When we have problems or emotional issues in our lives that we cannot understand sometimes we seek outside help. We may seek help from a: counselor, therapist, psychologist, Psychiatrist, religious/spiritual leader, family member, friend, or significant other. When we seek these individuals for help we openly communicate, we have emotional integrity, and we have humility. We tell them exactly what we are feeling/thinking so they can help us. Why does it take an individual outside of us to understand our emotions and thoughts? When we are the only people who are connected to our individual experiences; when we are the people who have first hand knowledge of the emotional response to an experience.

You may think that communicating to yourself may sound crazy. How do you think we motivate ourselves? How do you think we possess self-confidence? How do you think we possess self-esteem? How do you think we prioritize? We communicate to ourselves all the time, so we shouldn't treat our emotions or personal problems any different.

But then again we utilize people on the outside to give us a fresh perspective on our situations right? Sometimes an outside person can see something that we cannot see, due to us being inside the situation. On the other hand, doesn't it always take us to realize for ourselves what the outside person's perspective is? You have probably heard the saying before, "I can talk to you until I'm blue in the face, but it takes you to see it for yourself." The concept is the exact same for when our parents gave us advice. Our parents might have told us, "I'm telling you now don't do..." or "If you make the decision to...then...will happen."

So what happened, we made the decision that our parents warned us not to, and we fell flat on our face. It took for us to fall flat on our face before we could understand what our parents meant. The whole point of what I'm trying to convey is we create an extra step by seeking answers on the outside. At the end of the day, we are the ones who have to reach a self- realization point, in order to understand our emotions and thoughts. It is like we go outside to seek answers and we automatically get redirected to the inside of us. Say for instance you want to lose weight so you sign-up for a gym membership. A few weeks have passed and you have not seen any changes. So you ask yourself "What I am doing wrong, I still cannot lose weight." So you say "Maybe it's my diet; so you implement a diet that is consistent with your goal." You still notice that you're not losing weight, so you purchase a book on how to lose weight.

The whole time you have been focused on seeking outside help to reach your goal. The problem for you is that inside you did not have: motivation, consistency, patience and discipline.

You see, the problem wasn't outside it was inside. Now you can take what's on the inside and combine it with the variables on the outside to achieve your goal of losing weight. Once again do not get wrapped around the axle on relevance, I focus on concepts and the "Big Picture; while "Society" focuses on the "Little Picture" and being bass-ackwards.

When I was younger I went to a child psychologist. I remember my psychologist giving me worksheets to answer at home to help me to work out my issues. Guess what? The worksheets consisted of "6 question-words" about my life and I had to answer them honestly. Yes, you can see a psychologist for $X,XXX/hour to understand the human mind and to hear that theoretical nonsense. However, when it comes down to the practical issues in our lives, it always comes back to the inside of us. So instead, how about we just address our own emotions and thoughts right from the start. ALL OF THE SO-CALLED "RELATIONSHIP-EXPERTS",

RADIO SHOW HOST, MARRIAGE COUNSELORS, AND THOSE WITH THE PH.D'S ARE COMPLETELY CLUELESS!! PLEASE STOP SENDING YOUR MONEY TO THEM. INSTEAD, SAVE AND GO ON A VACATION WHERE YOU CAN COUNSEL YOURSELF ON A BEACH WITH "WHY- QUESTIONING". I was not yelling and am not angry with those above; I just believe they have been putting men and women on a collision course.

Do not allow your judgment, fear, or what

"Society" says prevent you from understanding who you are as an individual. There are too many people depending on "Society" for answers while we hold the answers and the tools inside of us. Our ability to possess emotional integrity contributes to building the framework for our individual foundation.

Communication! Communication!

If there is any quality or characteristic of a healthy relationship that should be at the top of the list, it's communication. Some of us actually think that we can build a relationship without communicating; good luck with that.

As human beings we have the capacity to communicate in multiple ways. Think about it, in verbal communication we have over one thousand languages in the world. With a plethora of dialects within each spoken language. For those of us who have hearing impairments we have the ability to communicate through sign language or lip reading. Today we're living in a tech savvy world, especially when it comes to non-verbal communication. We have the ability to send text messages and e-mails from our phones or computers. Also, we cannot forget the old fashion hand-written letters! Due to the constant advancements in technology we have the ability to use web cameras to enable us to communicate from a distance.

Additionally and exclusively, as human beings we have the ability to communicate through the use of: eye contact, body language, and facial expressions. Yet with all these various ways of communicating to one another, we still face difficulties communicating in our relationships. Why?

When it comes to communication there are two things in a relationship that baffles me. First, when I'm interested in a woman she seems to have difficulty talking about herself, but no difficulty talking about someone else. Some people have it backwards; people should be duty-experts on themselves not other people. Secondly, when people have difficulty answering the whole question. Have you ever asked someone one question and you have to ask several follow-up questions, just to get a partial answer? Then repeat the process to receive a whole answer? One would think by knowing the various forms of communication, it would be extremely simple to communicate. So what is obstructing the flow of communication from one person to another?

First of all, communication is a two-part process: there is the transmitting part and then there is the receiving part. In other words there is someone who is speaking and there is someone who is listening. Just like many things in life communication is an art. Knowing when to speak and when to listen is a journey in itself.

Once again the ability to communicate begins with oneself. Being able to have integrity and admit when we have done something that merits an apology, falls under the self-communication category. Being able to learn from an experience and applying what we learned to our current or future experiences, falls under this category. Being able to address our emotions and being honest with ourselves, falls under this category. Being able to have self-confidence falls under this category. Being able to be objective falls under this category. This list continues, but I think you get the idea.

If we cannot openly communicate with ourselves then how is it right for us to expect others to communicate with us? Think about insecurities, those that can openly and honestly communicate with themselves do not have insecurities. People have insecurities when they're unable to analyze and communicate to themselves; it's like people fear what they may learn about themselves. Whenever people learn something about themselves they are given a choice to either make a change or stay the same.

In this case with insecurities, we can either change so we're no longer insecure or remain the same. Now, if we have more than one person stating that we are insecure, then that should be a red flag for us to turn inwards. Not saying that they are right or wrong, but we should definitely analyze our experiences that connect us to those that claim we're insecure. When we ignore the "Red Flags", we end up causing a lot of damage in our relationships, including our self-relationship. Once you identify what you're insecure about, you will be amazed by how your experiences are interconnected to that insecurity.

In this case with insecurities, we can either change so we're no longer insecure or remain the same. Now, if we have more than one person stating that we are insecure, then that should be a red flag for us to turn inwards. Not saying that they are right or wrong, but we should definitely analyze our experiences that connect us to those that claim we're insecure. When we ignore the "Red Flags", we end up causing a lot of damage in our relationships, including our self-relationship. Once you identify what you're insecure about, you will be amazed by how your experiences are interconnected to that insecurity.

There is no mistake here; I wanted this to sink in.

For example, in the past I had a few women state that I was distant in the relationships with them, which I couldn't understand how that happened. No matter how much we communicated to each other, they always felt there was a gap. When I noticed that there were three separate consecutive relationships with women, I said to myself "There must be something I'm missing, since these women don't know each other and they're all saying the same thing."

Anyways, one day I was invited to a cookout at my ex- girlfriend's sister's house. I remember socializing with the guys at the cookout while watching my ex play with her nephews. They were having a blast, and then my ex came up to me and said, "So how many kids do you want Maceo?" I replied "As many as God will allow". As I'm driving us back to her apartment, she's talking about how much she enjoys being an aunt and how she can't wait to have kids. Listening to her speak started to make me feel distant, I remember saying to myself,

"Now why in the heck do I feel distant?" After dropping her off and driving home I'm still asking myself, "Why do I feel this way, why am I the one that feels distant now? I spent the whole day with her, so I started going through the sequence of events and all the conversations that we had. I noticed that I only felt distant when she was talking about having kids. Then the light bulb finally went off and I realized why I felt distant.

Several years prior I was diagnosed with a

medical condition that doesn't allow me to reproduce. In retrospect and out of all honesty, I remembered that when my previous ex-girlfriends were talking about having children that's when I put a distance between them and myself. Through continually asking myself "Why" and communicating to myself, I arrived at a reason.

The reason I was distant was because I was fearful of the relationship moving in the direction towards having children. That answer made a lot of sense but I still was not satisfied, and I wanted to know what was the real reason I was in fear. Sometimes we tell ourselves "Just enough" so we do not have to dig any deeper; in fact some of us actually do it with other people. It took a lot of self-analysis, honesty and "Why- questions" for me to understand what I really feared.

I feared falling in love with a woman and her not wanting to be in relationship with me because I couldn't have children. I feared never meeting a woman that would be okay with knowing that I couldn't have children. I used to get agitated when women would say, "Maceo you would make a great father one day". I would say "Thank You", but inside it frustrated me. It was frustrating knowing that the gift of life, was something that I couldn't participate in. As I continued to live, I came to a realization that there is more to life than just having children.

Eventually, as time passed I learned to embrace it and to be secure with myself. In the future whenever I went out on dates with women, I let them know right upfront that I couldn't reproduce. So down the road, if the topic came up, they would already know. It was kind of funny on my end; the beginning of my dates went like this:

"Hey, I'm glad we could get together, just so you know I can't reproduce..."

Anyways, let's take a closer look at the sequence of events:

1. By paying attention to my previous experiences (Relationships) and noticing the similarities (Red Flags) I became intrigued.

2. I noticed that I was feeling how my ex-girlfriends felt.

3. I began the inwards journey of "Why-questioning".

4. I reached an answer and the "fear" word surfaced.

5. I felt that answer was "Just Enough", but not enough.

6. I kicked my honesty level up a notch.

7. I analyzed my experiences with my ex-girlfriends (self-analysis).

8. I finally was honest enough with myself to understand what I really feared.

So I went from three relationships with three different women that made observations; to learning that beneath all of my experiences laid a fear that was affecting my relationships. I went from being insecure, to being secure through self-communication and analysis.

Now, remove your pride aside and start asking yourself questions.

How many people have said you're insecure?
_____

What did he or she say you were insecure about?

_____

_____

_____

_____

Take a step back, zoom out, and observe your experiences as if they were imprinted on a globe. When you reflect on your past relationships, do you notice that people are saying the same things about you? Yes or no? If no, reread the sentence above. If it's your second time rereading, marinate on the question. If yes, what are they?

_____

_____

Which experiences can you connect with the similarities?

_____

_____

_____

_____

_____

_____

_____

_____

Being able to effectively communicate can be difficult at times. We have to articulate our thoughts in a manner that the other person can receive it. We cannot control how someone receives what we say, but we can control how we speak to him or her. Some people either do not know how to communicate or are hesitant due to previous experiences with communicating their thoughts and feelings. Open communication between two people is like a highway; there should be lanes open from both ends of the highway to ensure that every vehicle of information gets to the opposite end. However, there are some highways that have obstacles that obstruct the flow of traffic and cause a standstill or make you take an unexpected detour.

Several years ago when I was in the military I used to be in a relationship with a woman that had traffic jams from her end to my end. Leah (Not her real name) had the most difficulty opening up to me and telling me her feelings. It was like pulling teeth when it came to communication. I had to constantly ask questions to pull bits of information out of her. I used to get so frustrated and angry because I couldn't understand how Leah couldn't express herself. I wasn't talking about Leah telling me about someone else; I was talking about Leah telling me about Leah. One day I asked her "Why is it so hard to talk to me?" She said, "I don't know, I never had to be so open before." Of course in my head I was saying, "If you don't know, then who knows?" But she was able to communicate that answer to me, so it was a start.

After our brief conversation, I was doing some thinking on how I could help to open up the lanes and an idea popped in my head. The idea came from the concept of progress reports and report cards in school. So I brought the idea to Leah's attention, "I have an idea that can help us in the communication department. Every two weeks or so I'll ask you how you think the relationship is going. You can tell me your thoughts like: if you think I can improve or if I say or do things that you don't like or if anything you're feeling. This way we can avoid the Snowball effect". The snowball effect happens when someone doesn't release his or her thoughts and feelings. The end result, is a situation in which every thought and feeling comes out usually in the form of an emotional outburst.

Every single time someone does not address his or her emotions, five things happen:

1. Implode and how you view self goes out the window.

2. Explode and direct your emotions outwards.

3. The emotions stay in and eat you up until you cannot function.

4. You attract experiences that will allow the emotions to surface for healing (Which counteract if you refuse to address the emotions;

thus, repeating the same cycle of experiences with or without the same individuals involved).

5. Fluctuate between 1-4.

Why put yourself through it? Why hold on to unaddressed emotions? Holding back your feelings and/or thoughts does not improve your self-relationship or your relationship with someone else.

I know there is someone thinking right now "Every time I release my thoughts and/or feelings, it doesn't improve my relationship. So I rather keep them in." Well here are four words for you, good luck with that! Eventually, Leah got comfortable with communicating to me about how she felt. What we did was not the "traditional" way, but it worked. Sometimes in relationships, you have to improvise and do what works best for the both of you. The communication difficulties that I had with Leah were relatively smoother compared to Sara (Not her real name). Sara was the type of a woman who I had to constantly express to her that I was not her ex-boyfriend.

Her ex-boyfriend must have been a tool because there were no vehicles on her lane. Sara used to be in a relationship with a man who verbally abused her whenever she communicated how she felt. Which makes perfect sense why she wouldn't communicate to me. However, why enter a new relationship with someone, knowing you cannot communicate? That is like buying a new car knowing you do not have a driver's license. What's the point?

Having gone through the communication issue with Leah, I had way more patience when it came to Sara. If there are issues in your past that hinder your ability to communicate to yourself, then there will be issues when it comes to communicating to someone else. Everything in life is interconnected.

Fear Blocks the Flow of Love

As I stated earlier Sara had issues talking to me because of fear of how I would react, which was because of her previous boyfriend. Fear is a beast that destroys everything. There is no special trick or any one-time cure that will destroy fear. We have to make an effort to move beyond fear. Fear has the ability to dominate every aspect of our lives, especially when it comes to relationships. Fear is like a leech and once it attaches to an experience or us it stays there continuing to feed off of us.

When fear attaches itself to some aspect of our lives, that fear becomes a part of us and we end up getting in our own way. In order to get out of our own way, we have to lose our minds. Our mind is where the fear rests. Fear and love cannot co-exist. If there is fear, then there is no love; if there is love, then there is no fear. Love is positive energy and fear is negative energy, they are opposites. We cannot love with emotions that stem from worry and fears of the unknown. Ask yourself this, how can someone love with fears of "What-if...?" How can someone love him or herself if he or she is full of fear? If you live in fear of your heart being broken, how can you love someone? How can someone love with doubts, which ultimately stem from fear? I often wonder how people can fear God and love God at the same time, when fear blocks the flow of love.

So if you're looking for a scapegoat, fear is where the finger should be pointed. Since fear attached itself to you, then you are pointing the finger at yourself. We create our fears when we worry about the future and if we want to eliminate fear, we have to live in the "Now." When we live in the "Now" it's impossible to live in fear of the future because what's happening in the moment is all there is. Technically, the "Now" is all we have so why spend your time in fear of the unknown, in fear of what could happen? If you really think about it, a lot of us spend so much time replaying the past and thinking about the future. It really makes you wonder who is actually "Here". (One of my foundational questions from Ex.2 Human Beings-Physical)

When people create fears they also create the emotions that go along with the fears. No different than someone thinking positively about his or her future and producing the correct mindset with positive emotions. So if one person produces one thought of fear of the future, he or she also produces the necessary emotions that are attached to fear. It is like our thoughts send a message to the multiple levels of our being, for preparation to move in the direction of our thoughts. Our reality is based on our thoughts. Fears not only create fear-based emotions they also create anxieties. With each creation of fear, an individual is creating walls of fear that take the form of a box. Inside this box is a window that allows the individual to be warned of what/who is coming his or her way. To the individual this box is for protection from the outside; when the individual inside the box causes the most harm.

Fear itself comes down to a loss of control in our lives. Let's take cheating for example, if you could control how the future played out, you wouldn't go into a relationship full of fear would you? Fear comes down to control. As soon as you come to a self-realization that you have no control over the future, fear immediately goes out the window. And I'm talking about in seconds.

Our fears stem from the inability to receive an outcome of an experience in a timely manner. Meaning the "Waiting Game" of not knowing stimulates the fears inside of us. The "Waiting Game" is best known for, "I wonder if..." or "I hope..."

I think people do not want to be caught off guard by being unprepared for what's in front of them. In some people's mind creating fear allows them to protect themselves from being hurt. So when something does happen people can say, "I knew it" or "I knew that would happen, I'm so glad I did not put myself out there." It is these same people who allow fear to dictate their lives and find themselves often wondering about their relationships. Those of you who fear the past becoming the future, ultimately end up with the "Now" being the past. Thus, your reality is in the past; hence why you enter a relationship full of fear. Learn from the past then release it, live in the "Now", and accept that the future is to be determined.

When we think we are over the fears we say, "That's all in the past, I'm ready for a relationship" or "I learned from the experience, I'm ready now", but fear is what stops us from communicating. As soon as it's time for us to communicate to our significant other, our mouth opens and no words come out.

We stop like a deer in the middle of the road staring at headlights. The best way to tell if you learned from an experience is from what you do with the knowledge from your learning lesson. There are people who say all the time that they have learned from an experience, but when faced with another experience, they slip back into their old groove. Therefore, he or she did not learn from his or her experience. When you learn from an experience you are able to apply that knowledge to your future experiences. When the knowledge is applied, is when knowledge turns into wisdom.

Back to my example about being insecure of my inability to reproduce, I used to have fears of being in a relationship because of not knowing how a woman would react. That fear obstructed the flow of communication. I wouldn't let women get to know me due to fear of really liking them and the relationship not working. I know you may say, "Well that's different, it's medically related." Fear is fear, it doesn't matter the weight or size of fear it still causes damage both internally and externally.

If you cannot communicate because of fears of "Putting yourself out there" and getting hurt, then ask yourself why. Is that what you really fear? Or is that you fear feeling the same way you did the last times you tried to communicate? Maybe the last time you attempted to communicate your significant other might have belittled you. So every time you want to communicate, the first thought that pops into your mind is being belittled. So you say to yourself, "I really don't need to say that" or "We can get through this without me saying what I feel".

On one side of the spectrum we have the power to create our fears, so what does that mean? We have the power to dismantle and release ourselves from the fears. The same process that we used to create the fears is the same process that we must use to wipe the fears out. When you understand what your fears are, you take the power away from them. Fear is created in the mind. Picture your fears as bullets; if you take the gunpowder out, the bullets are useless. Make sense?

How do you release yourself from fear? First, you must identify your fears with integrity. Secondly, ask yourself why you have those fears. Lastly, you must realize for yourself that the future is dependent on what is thought and done in the "Now". Stop worrying about the future or even the past. Meaning stop worrying about if the future will be just like your past. Accept the fact that your experiences are lessons to help you grow on multiple levels. When you implement this perspective in your life; your stress levels go down tremendously. Our ability to address our emotions is what helps us to learn our individual lessons. We cannot learn our lessons when fear is in the way. Which is probably why a few of us have repetitive relationships because we have not faced our fears. What exactly is the point of going into a relationship with fear in the mind?

I have dated women who attempted to have a relationship with me with fear in the mind along with problems communicating. That has to be the worst combination ever; they could not move forward and they could not tell me why. In case you are wondering it is very simple to detect fear. If you are on a date and your significant other is not "Here" then there is fear present. Worry, anxious, jealousy, is also attached to fear. I stated earlier that the fears that some of us have are linked to our past experiences.

Our past relationships may have been full of

"Emotional roller coasters" or "Sad-emotions". These "Emotional roller coasters" or "Sad-emotions" are based on how we perceive the experiences before our eyes. So the people who have these fears are the same people who are fearful going into a relationship. Do you see how our fears are interconnected to how we perceive an experience?

Shift Your Perspective

However, when we are able to shift our perspective on an experience something else happens. Imagine there are two individuals who just got out of a relationship. The first person's emotions go completely out of control. One day he or she is happy and "Moving on"; the next day he or she is down and really wants to get back with his or her ex-significant other. This person constantly goes over the relationship in his or her head to figure out what happened. This person really took an emotional hit and vows to never let him or herself get hurt again. Right about now is when the fears start to manifest.

Also, this is when the self-evaluation comes in, "How could I be so stupid to believe..." Over time this person has created and fed his or her fears, so when the next opportunity comes he or she will have fear in the way of the future relationship. It is a viscous cycle that needs to be broken. If this person does not address his or her emotions then the emotions end up turning into fears.

On the other side, is the other person who had a different perspective on the breakup. This person got emotional too, but decided to shift his or her perspective while addressing the emotions. In a sense this person takes a step back and observes the relationship as a whole. While doing this, he or she is able to absorb the lessons, which are beneath the surface. Emotions that are out of control tend to blind us from the learning lessons that are within the experiences. The lessons that he or she learns from the relationship outweigh the emotions alone, 100% of the time. It is the lessons that enable a person to grow on multiple levels and aids him or her in the future.

When we fail to learn the lessons because of our emotions being out of control and not addressing them, we end up repeating the lesson over and over again. Unaddressed Emotions without the learning lesson create fear and anxiety because you only see what's on the surface. In other words, you only see what caused you to get emotional, you cannot see beneath the surface where the learning lesson is. Addressed Emotions with the learning lesson do not create fear or anxiety because you understand why you went through that experience. You do not have to wait five years in order for you to understand why you went through an experience. If you shift your perspective, you will learn the lesson in minutes, instead of years.

Arguments

Arguments or disagreements whichever you prefer to call them happen in relationships. Arguments are like "Merry-go- rounds", you go round and round in the same area of space. Once the "Merry-go-round" is done, you've become so disoriented that you have no idea where you got on the ride. In other words, our arguments have the tendency to go back and forth for a while that we end up losing focus on what "sparked" the argument.

Have you ever been in an argument and reached a point where you ask yourself or your significant other, "Why are we arguing again?" When that question are ones along that line arises, you need to put yourself an "Emotional Check" mode. When we get in those "Heated" arguments in which sweat is pouring down our face or we can hear our heart beating at ninety-percent of our max heart rate; our emotions are out of control. Thus, you need to check your emotions at the door before another word comes out of your mouth.

Our emotions go haywire because of the energy that the other is projecting in the tone and words of what he or she is saying. I'll get more in depth on that type of energy in my next book. A few of us feel hurt by the words so we feel compelled to "Get back" at him or her by using words to hurt them. The cycle of hurtful words continues until someone crosses "The line". I'm sure you know what the line is, in case you do not know; it's the point of no return. Meaning once you cross "The line", you cannot take anything back. Unfortunately, some people choose to cross that line with physical force or what I think is even worse, soul-piercing words. Personally, I believe words can cause more damage because of the lasting affect that it can produce.

When the argument is done and people cannot reach an agreement, people either go their separate ways willingly or by the assistance of police officers. Now, when the two individuals come back to talk they say their apologies for what was said during the argument and explain how they didn't mean to say...On that note, I cannot understand why people say that they didn't mean to say something in an argument. If you didn't mean to say something, then you wouldn't have said it. If you said something, then you meant it. What I find funny is how no one can remember what started the argument, but can remember every single hurtful word or action that happened because of the argument.

For the longest in relationships, I used to argue back and forth with women. What really made me angry was how women in my past would say something, then minutes later, say that they didn't say something. I was always like "Do you listen to the words when you say them because I sure do."

Leah as you remember, had a problem with communication when we first started dating. The inability for her to communicate to me caused a lot of "Sparks" for arguments. Anyone that has been in my shoes knows that's like running into a brick wall over and over again. Which further proves my point; you need communication in a relationship! If you have not been in my shoes, then hopefully you will not ever be in those shoes.

I remember one day almost like it was yesterday, well maybe it was a few years ago. Anyways, Leah and I went down to the beach to walk on the boardwalk. We were walking and decided to stop at one of the snowball vendors. Leah put her order in as well as myself. When the vendor whom was a female, told us the price, I handed her the money. I said, "Where are you from, I hear an accent?" The vendor said, "I'm from Russia I came her for the summer." I said, "Oh that's nice, are you liking it over here?" She said, "Yea I'm having fun." While she was handing me my change I said, "Thank you and enjoy the rest of your visit."

Meanwhile I look over my shoulder and Leah took off ahead of me. When I caught up to her I said, "Leah why are you walking so fast?" She turned her head and just looked at me. I said, "What?" She didn't say anything. So I gave her the snowball that she ordered and we continued walking on the boardwalk. We ended up staying down at the beach for dinner before we left.

When we got inside the car, I noticed her face was looking like she was irritated. So I asked, "What's wrong?" Again, she didn't say anything. I said, "I know something is wrong, so what is it?" She said, "Nothing is wrong Maceo." I said "Okay", as I was backing out of the parking space I told her that I needed to drop off some movie rentals and ask a question about my account before I drop her off. When we pulled into the parking lot of Blockbuster I said, "Do you want to come in or stay in the car?" Leah said, "Why stay in the car, so you can talk to that girl behind the counter", as she pointed through the windshield. I got out the car, dropped my rentals in the movie box and got back in the car. I told her, "I'll call them about my account later. I'm sure glad nothing is wrong with you."

When I used to get frustrated with people I used to become the biggest Smart Alec. Since trying to get a visitors car on base used to be a hassle, Leah used to park her car in the shopping center across from the base and I would pick her up from there to bring her on base. I pulled right up to her car and said, "Thank you for choosing Maceo's taxi services, please exit and have a safe trip home". Leah just sat there; I was getting angry with her not talking about whatever was on her mind. Then she said, "You're a flirt". I asked, "How am I a flirt?"

She just sat there. "Ya know I get so tired of this crap, this off and on; you speak and then you just shutdown. Why do you do that? You might as well have not said anything. Again, Thank you for choosing Maceo's taxi services please exit and have a safe trip." Then Leah said, "Why are you getting angry with me?" I rolled down the windows and turned the ignition off then told her, "Well let's see, hmmm, maybe because you're not opening up. How about you be a big girl and tell me what you're feeling." She then said "So you're calling me a child now huh?" "No not at all, children are fearless they say exactly what they think.

You on the other hand may be closer to a newborn, since they have no clue how to articulate their feelings." "You see Maceo, this is why it's so hard to talk to you." I turned off the radio and said, "What are you talking about? I'm angry because I don't know why you can't say what's on your mind. So I guess we will just sit her until you say something.

Leah replied, "Something." Under my breath I said, "I sure wonder what it is like to be single, the way things are looking now I may not have to wonder anymore." That comment pushed me closer to "The Line", and that's when the yelling match began. We went back and forth for a while sitting in the empty parking lot. It ended with Leah getting out, slamming my door, and me going back to base.

Approximately a week or so passed and I sent her text saying we need to talk. It took her two days to reply back to the text message. Leah replied with the infamous "K". So I sent her text back asking her if she wanted to meet in the parking lot across the base. She said, "No, but we can meet in the parking lot at the park near my house." So I drove to the park and pulled my car up to hers.

I rolled down my window and asked her, "Do you want me to sit in your car or do you want me to sit in yours?" She told me she wanted me to sit in hers. When I got in the car I asked her how she was doing and she said she was okay. I said in a very calm tone, "Look, I'm sorry for getting angry and not having more patience with you. But it really irks my nerves when you can't open up and talk to me." Lean then said, "I'm sorry too Maceo, but I am trying to open up more." "Okay, so we're still together right?" She said, "Yeah that hasn't changed." I said, "Phew you had me scared there all week. So now since we are having a calm conversation, can you tell me what was on your mind last week"?

"I absolutely knew you would say that", Leah told me. "Well then you must know me better that I thought." "When we went to the snowball stand, I felt like you were flirting with the snowball lady." I interrupted and said, "Flirting?" "Wait, I'm not finished. I felt that you sorta ignored me to talk to the girl at the snowball stand. Over this past week I thought about us and realized that you just like to talk. It's a part of your personality." "Leah, I like you a lot; you're not the only woman that thought I was a flirt. I really don't mean to come across as a flirt; I just like talking to people."

Chapter 5. Internal Vs. External View

A healthy relationship in which two individuals are connected beneath the surface is what so many of us are eager to find. However, the ways in which we determine compatibility are not congruent with a healthy relationship. There are a lot of people who are suffering due to the compatibility issues that we find down the road. **Our perception of what we think is priority one in a relationship, is actually priority two.** Which is why we still run into unhealthy relationships and feel like no matter what we do we get the same results. For example, some of us think finding a man or woman who is ambitious is considered priority one; while, finding a man or woman who has a career/job is priority two or vice versa.

When in fact, these two examples are still on the surface, thus the reason for getting the same results. Always remember no matter what we change on the surface; we will get the same results. As soon as we realize that the surface is not priority one, our perception of relationships will change drastically; as well as our perception of life. Below the surface is priority one and where your foundational questions take root. Above the surface is priority two and where your surface questions are. At this point you must be curious to know what priority one and two are right?

Priority one is the building blocks for the foundation and is the essence of what makes you who you are. It is the combination of your perception of life, definition of happiness, emotional integrity, wisdom from life experiences, ethics, and life principles in which your life is rooted. What falls under this category is constantly a part of your life; it does not matter the day of the week, or what surrounds you externally. What's inside you is something that no one can take from you, it's engraved in your spirit.

Priority two is what many people think is priority one; in a sense it is the complete opposite, meaning priority two is like seasons (they come and go). Priority two is composed of: goals, financial stability, strength and weakness, favorite foods, common hobbies, music, movies, sports, favorite colors, employment status, education level, favorite novels, etc. Also, questions like:

Where do you see yourself five years from now? Are you willing to relocate to...? Do not get me wrong priority two has it roles; it's just not the main focus, and it's definitely not the building blocks for a foundation.

As far as physical attraction goes, it plays a role. To those that believe "Looks do not matter; it's what's inside that matters", once again they do play a role believe it or not. If you see someone from a distance you do not say "Looks like he or she has one heck of a conscientious". Physical attraction can bring two people together, but the words that come out of his or her mouths determine if they stay together.

I have dated quite a few women over the years and the majority of them had the priority categories mixed up. I do not blame the women; I blame the so-called "Relationship Experts of Society" including the Ph. D's. I ran in to friction in my previous relationships because of the perception issue. In retrospect it was very frustrating being the only one that had this perspective. At one point I started questioning myself on the validity of my perspective. Once I realized that my perspective on relationships is consistent with my perception of life, I stopped asking myself questions.

Whenever I meet women I'm always asked, "What are you looking for? Are you looking for anything serious? Or casual? I'm not looking for a girlfriend, a future wife, etc. The keyword is "Looking"; I'm not looking for anything. I'm living my life and enjoying the journey. Now, if I cross paths with someone else, it doesn't change anything; I'll still start with a conversation. I accept the fact that I have no control for what the future holds and I realize that everything starts with a conversation.

I love mental stimulation through conversation so a conversation dictates the future for me. Technically, a conversation dictates the future for everyone. So what everyone should be focused on is the conversation. By living in the "Now" we can learn a lot within our conversations. When we're "Looking", we're living in the future. We are thinking, "Will this person be my future...?" When we do that we lose our focus on what is happening in the "Now". Some of us get ahead of ourselves due to being impatient and wanting a significant other. Before one word is even spoken some of us have started to manifest feelings because we may want a person to be "The one". When this happens, it becomes difficult to differentiate between these feelings and whether or not we are actually connecting with another person. So, live in the "Now" and start off with a conversation.

Connecting beneath the surface is what enables two individuals to build and develop a healthy relationship. This is the relationship that most people visualize. People can utilize what is at their foundation (Priority one) to determine compatibility with someone else. In a sense, you use what's at your foundation to form questions and great conversation when you meet someone. Hence, why it's so important to know what's at your foundation. Without connecting beneath the surface, you end up with very shallow relationships; ones that probably make you say, "Why can't I ever have a real relationship?"

I would rather connect with a woman at her foundation and have nothing on the surface in common; than having commonalities on the surface and not connecting at the foundation. Priority one is like the main meal and priority two is like the side dishes. We're content with the main meal and can do without all the sides. However, we cannot get full off of just the side dishes. When we do have just the side dishes, we still feel like something is missing. Makes sense right?

If you have children, obviously they are going to be a part of your foundation. So I imagine your children are going to be a part of that initial conversation with whom you meet.

Your children are a part of your life and if someone isn't compatible with you because of your children, forget about them. If he or she says that their life doesn't have any room for children, thank him or her for being honest and keep it moving. Do not stay with them because you connect with him or her on so many levels and you think you can change his or her mind. Remember always stay true and real to yourself; you shouldn't have to change one thing or mold someone into the man or woman that you like.

Christina attempted to mold me into a man that she wanted. I have a crazy hairline; it looks like a NIKE check, when my hair grows in. I like to mix up it up when it comes to my haircut and facial hair. Christina started off saying; "I think you would look better if you changed your haircut." I knew exactly where she was going with that, so I played along to see how far she was going to go. I shaved my goatee off one day prior to our date at the movie and she didn't like that. So she said, "You look better with the goatee, you should never shave your face again." Then she looked at my shoes saying I'd look better in some weird looking duck boots. Christina was obviously trying to change me, but I'm not changing for anyone and definitely not for Society.

Discriminators

Have you ever noticed that the last few people you dated were all the same? So, you asked yourself "What am I doing wrong or what should I do differently to avoid dating men or women like this"? If we ask those that are in our "Bubble" they may say, "The problem is the type of men or women you're attracting and once you realize that, you won't run into anymore issues".

So you probably noticed a common trait or characteristic between the men or women you've dated and you told yourself in the future you're dating someone who is the complete opposite or...As human beings, we are inquisitive by nature that's why we have the tendency to want to figure out what we are doing wrong in regards to our relationships. When we analyze our relationships we have the tendency to associate specific characteristics that ultimately form labels. Labels do not exist take maturity for instance. Maturity is a common characteristic that people attempt to find and I'm sorry to tell you this, it will not be found until our physical bodies are laid to rest. By definition to be mature means that one is fully developed.

There are three (Four if you break down the mental aspect) aspects to human beings: the mental aspect (intellect & emotions), the physical aspect, and the spiritual aspect. Our emotional state changes like the weather; so technically we can "Re-develop" emotions at any time. As far as intellect goes, we are constantly learning so our intellect is constantly evolving. Whether we are learning the lessons of life or learning a particular topic/subject. Being fully developed physically is dependent on the individual.

Height wise a person can reach a certain age and realize that he or she has stopped growing vertically. However, if a person increases or decreases muscle strength or size, then that person is not fully developed physically are they? If a person loses weight or gains weight he or she is not fully developed are they? Due to the technical nature of the physical aspect, people are either 0/3 or 1/3 developed (3 aspects of physical development-Height, Muscle, & Weight). On the spiritual aspect, if we were fully developed spiritually then we would not be in the physical form.

Death of the physical form is the only way to

be mature (Fully developed). All that is left is the spirit; the physical form (body) and the mental form (intellect & emotions) are left behind. Therefore, the spirit is mature (fully developed); the spirit is 1/1 because the spirit is all there is. So "Society" should probably remove the word "Mature" from every dictionary and thesaurus. But since "Society" enjoys misleading people, it will most likely stay in there.

Once again, "Society" including "Relationship-Experts" have no idea what they are talking about. We are constantly learning and growing so you will never find someone who is mature or perfect until it is time to go home. Have you ever really thought about the word "Perfect"? The word seems to be circling every relationship and everything else in life. If we are always learning, how can anyone be perfect? On that note, how can anyone be a master of anything? To be perfect or a master, you have learned everything and there is no need for improvement. I have never met anyone who was perfect or a master of anything in life. I was born in America and English is my first and primary language. I have Native-fluency in English; however, I'm still learning new vocabulary words each day. I have not perfected or mastered the American-English language. A wise individual knows that everything can be fine-tuned and there is always room for improvement.

Take martial arts for instance, there are some who believe that starting with no belt and reaching a black belt, means they are at the top of their game. On the other side of the spectrum, there are those who believe the black belt is where the training really begins. The words "Perfect" or "Master" do not exist. Once again, "Society", including the Ph. D's are lost in the sauce. In academia there is the "Master's Degree Program"; you need to obtain this degree in order to obtain your Ph. D right? I just broke down the words "Perfect, master, and mature", so what does that tell you about the credibility of a Ph. D? Are you still with me?

Moving on... Say we notice that the last few men or women we dated didn't have a job or career; and we did have a job or career. We may tell ourselves, "The last men or women didn't have a job/career, so that's why he or she didn't understand about: having priorities, being goal oriented, and being financially stable, etc". So we say, "The next time I date a man or woman he or she must have a job/career in order to date me". We ended up associating characteristics like priorities, goals, and financial stability to job/careers. Thinking that if an individual has a job or career, they'll possess these characteristics. Well, that's not always the case right? So what do we do next?

We repeat the same analysis, except we may ask someone else for his or her opinion or someone else may volunteer his or her opinion for us. Sometimes those that are on the outside can see things about us that we cannot see for ourselves, that's why we ask for their help. So he or she may say, "You're a man or woman of God and the problem is, all your past relationships are with men or women that didn't put God first. So what you need to do is find a 'Church going' man or woman". So we say to ourselves, "That's right! Then he or she will have: faith, patience, compassion, morals, etc". Once again, we would love to believe that all men and women who put God first have the above characteristics, but not all do. Especially when it comes to morals.

Do not misinterpret my words, I'm focusing on what characteristics that we make associations with. Of course people want a quick way to assess an individual and complete that check in the box for morals. When it comes to qualities such as morals, there is no easy way out to determine if someone has morals. You find out if someone has morals through observation and listening. One of the beauties about morals is that actions speak a heck of a lot louder than words. Anyone can say that he or she has morals, but his or her actions will tell you even better.

Observing how a person handles his or her experiences and the choices that he or she makes in life will show you if they have morals. Also, by listening to a person telling you about his or her life lessons and listening to the words that are spoken to you.

Possessing morals is not one of the qualities that you can easily make word associations with and complete a check-in-a-box. Good ole fashioned conversation can tell you a lot about a person, if people can have the patience to have face-to-face conversations and not through text messaging. Text messages do not include facial expressions, eye contact, tone and energy.

Do not forget, we are inquisitive beings, we

love to think outside the box and try to understand what we are doing wrong to attract certain type of men or women. Maybe we think to ourselves, that it's probably the locations in which we're meeting these people. So the next time we go out in town, we "Switch it up" as in which locations we go to mingle. Say that the last three failed relationships we had were from meeting people in bars and/or nightclubs. Instead of going to those places, we decide to go to a place with a different atmosphere. We meet a man or woman and we notice that the person is different from who we are "Usually attracted to".

So we say, "All this time it was the locations of the men or women that I was attracting". Some time has passed, and we realize we are not compatible with the person. This is when the mental fatigue kicks in and we become frustrated with ourselves, not being able to have a healthy relationship. The conclusion that we reach is there is no man or woman for me. We lose hope for relationships, love, and in men or women. We realize that it's not the locations and/or the type of men or women because of dating a variety of men or women. At the same time, we have no clue as in what we're missing or where the problem lies. We ask questions like: what the heck is wrong with me; why are all men... why are all women...?

At this point we reach a fork in the road, on one side we say along the lines of "Forget about relationships and finding a man/woman. I'm focusing on me, if someone is interested he or she has to make it really clear; I'm done putting myself out there and getting hurt". On the other side we say along the lines of "I'm missing something; there has to be a man/woman out there for me." On this side of the road, the person uses the same analysis but makes some changes to the associations and/or locations (Surface).

Perception plays an important role in our lives and everything in life begins with us. Perhaps the problems that we face with our relationships are due to what we perceive to be the problem. As I stated in the previous chapters some of us have the "Outward" focus in our lives. When we analyze our past relationships we ask, "What do the men or women have in common?"

We arrive at answers that relate to characteristics/ traits that we perceive to be the issues with our past relationships. Instead of looking "Outward" we need to look "Inward" first. When we do that and we ask the same question, "What do the men or women have in common?" we get a different answer.

The answer we arrive at is, we are what's in common. We are what connects us to all of our past relationships. You are the common denominator in every single experience you have ever faced. When we shift our perspective from the external to the internal and focus our attention to being the common denominator, we embark on a quest of the inner self. Our inner self (foundation) has all the answers that we expected to be answered by focusing externally (surface).

No matter what we changed externally, some of us still felt like we were missing something. Our inner self or self-relationship is the missing piece to the puzzle.

However, this does not mean that all of our relationships from this point on will be a smooth. What this means, is that we can analyze our lives with clarity now and see the "Big Picture". This inner journey requires communication, patience, emotional integrity, and humility. If you notice, these are the same qualities that we look for in a relationship with someone else. There is no coincidence here this is the truth. Despite what you may have learned, everything in life begins with us and relationships are no different.

Usually those whom do not possess these qualities are the ones who have problems in relationships: when it comes to communicating, being patient, being honest with their emotions, and having humility over pride. We need to have humility within ourselves. When the humility level is higher compared to the pride level, we have a higher chance of shifting our perspective.

On the other hand, when our pride level is higher than our humility level, we have almost no chance of shifting our perspective. In this case shifting our perspective would be "Trying to understand where the other person is coming from". When our pride level is higher, we say along the lines of "I have done nothing wrong or it's not my fault".

For the longest time I've always had an issue in my relationships when it came to my conversations. A lot of the topics/subjects that were in my conversations were not very popular in my relationships. In fact many of my conversations sparked a lot of arguments. So I analyzed my past relationships and what I found in common and focused on was the age range. I thought to myself, "Maybe the age range is the reason why I cannot have an interesting conversation with women".

So of course I said, "For now on I'll only date women that are older than me by 5 or 10 years. At this age range, maybe they would find my topics/subjects more interesting". So I ended up dating a woman who was older than me by 8 years. I enjoyed our time together, but I still ran into a brick wall when it came to our conversations. After several more dates with older women I reached a conclusion, that age wasn't the issue.

The whole time I was focused externally on what all the women had in common. So, I decided to shift my perspective and focus on me being the common denominator. I focused on the conversations themselves and what was the common theme. I realized it wasn't the conversations that were the problem with my relationships. The problems stemmed from my perception of life, which were a central theme in my conversations. In other words, the subject matter for my conversations was based on my perception of life. I realized that my perception of life and my observations of life were at my foundation. I learned two important things about life in general and myself.

Our perceptions of life are like umbrellas;

our observations from every aspect of life are covered under our perceptions. Every decision we make in life, every experience we face, our emotional response to those experiences, and the quality of knowledge that was learned from our experiences, are all based on our perceptions of life. Therefore, if two people have different perceptions of life or one does not have a perception of life, then the two individuals will run into a lot of issues. Learning this about life often makes me wonder if people are wandering around aimlessly.

As far as what I learned about myself, I now have one question from my foundation to ask women when I go on dates. The question is "What are your observations of life?" I can use this question to determine if a woman is compatible with me at the foundation level, beneath the surface. Instead of dating a woman for weeks, months, etc, and finding out the way she perceives life isn't compatible with me. Are you still with me?

Chapter 6. Foundation of Happiness

...Life, liberty, and the pursuit of happiness were what our founding fathers wanted for everyone. The pursuit of happiness seems to be very prevalent in society today. People pursue careers, wealth and relationships with the intention of receiving happiness upon arrival. You have heard people say, "I'll be happy when I..." The question is, "Do people obtain happiness once he or she arrives at..." Do these same people want someone to make them happy because they have always been sad in relationships?

Or is that people are born innately knowing that they must find happiness by being with a man or woman? There are quite a few people that are in pursuit of a man or woman that can make them happy. If I had a dollar for every time someone said they were looking for someone to make them happy, then I would have enough money to have self-published this book. So how does someone give someone everlasting happiness? You have to excuse me; I didn't mean to add everlasting happiness. There is a difference between everlasting happiness and "Happiness upon arrival".

I was picking my sister's brain not too long ago about herself and her relationships. I said "Any new prospects in the dating world for you?" She replied, "No, not right now, I'm talking to a guy right now, I tell you how that goes." So I asked her "What do you look for in guys when you're dating?" She said, "A guy must make me happy, make time for me, text me before I go to sleep; I should see his morning text when I wake up, you know?" "Actually I don't know that's why I asked." So I asked, "What happens if a guy doesn't make you happy?"

She said, "Then, we have nothing to talk about if a guy can't make me happy; then he can't get with me." I said, " That makes sense, but I am curious about something. What is your definition of happiness? What do you define as a guy making you happy?" She says, "Ummm, I never really thought about it like that." I said, "There is no other way to think about it." She replied, "I don't know how to define what happiness means". So I said, "So let me recap this convo; you look for a guy who can make you happy; but when I ask your definition of happiness, you can't answer it right?" She said, "Yea."

I said, "Now that makes no sense you're your looking for something that you can't define; something that you don't know the meaning to; something that you use as a gauge for determining whether or not a guy can be with you. You remember in school when the teacher used to say do not use a word if you cannot define it? The same concept applies to relationships." Her reply was, "Look I don't have anytime for this Mackie (My family nickname), bottom-line; this is what I look for." I said, "Okay."

I love my sister to death and beyond, but she happens to fall in the category with a lot of people who are looking for men or women to make them happy. My sister is not the only person who had difficulty answering that question. What I find interesting is when I ask that question, people want to tell me what isn't the definition of happiness. I ask them and they say, "Happiness isn't when the person does...to me. Or when a person says...to me." Hearing these types of answers makes me wonder if people are associating these answers with happiness. Meaning that people subconsciously define happiness along these lines: as someone who doesn't make the other person sad, make the other person angry, someone who likes the person for whom they are, etc.

The question that rolls around in my head is, "If people can't define happiness, then what the heck are they looking for?" The conclusion that I arrived at was, that some people have no clue what they're looking for. I'm not talking about "People do not know what they want"; I'm talking about people "Going with the flow" in society, without every looking up and asking, "Where exactly am I going?" It's like society handed everyone a map with directions and no legend, so people just automatically got on the road and drove to a destination. Then when they arrived at the destination, they realized that it wasn't what it was all cracked up to be. People feel like they were shortchanged, so they get frustrated with themselves and begin the "Why-questioning". Before trying to determine if a man or woman can make you happy, how about asking yourself what being happy means; what do you as the individual define as happiness.

There are some people who believe happiness is an emotion, or a combination of emotion and a way of life. I think the people that look for a man or woman to make them happy are people who believe in happiness being an emotion. Think about it, if you're always being in relationships where you feel: sad, depressed, nervous, scared, or clueless, then it makes perfect sense to find someone that brings out the happiness emotion in you.

However, what if a person brings happiness in your life, but may make you sad or angry, does that mean you want out of the relationship? Hypothetically speaking, say there is a man or woman in a relationship who loves to be surprised with happy gestures of appreciation. This person believes that the person he or she is in a relationship with makes them really happy when they are spontaneous with gratitude. But lately, this person has noticed that the significant other hasn't been showing appreciation. Is it justifiable if this person breaks up with the other person for not making him or her happy?

Within every relationship (Types are irrelevant) there are times when a person can bring happiness, but there are also times when a person can bring frustration. Once again, having a balance in your life is important. If people are basing their relationships on the "Happiness" emotion alone, then it also makes sense why they feel they cannot find someone. You see the thing is, when you date someone with the intention of them making you happy all the time, you end up becoming dependent on that person.

Picture two walls parallel to each other and one wall decides to lean on the other; if that other wall moves in any direction, what happens to the wall that is leaning? The other wall falls straight to the ground. It's fine and dandy to enjoy happiness that someone brings into your life, but not depend on him or her to make you happy. One of the problems is that there are too many men and women that only experienced unhealthy relationships. So he or she sets out in the dating world with the objective of only dating someone that can make him or her happy. I wonder if there is a connection here with the divorce rate and people marrying the other person because he or she makes the other person happy. What do I know? I do not have a Ph. D in Sociology; all I have is a high school diploma.

On the other hand, there is the other type of happiness. I'm not talking about the type of happiness where you reach a certain age in your life and you can officially be happy now. I'm not talking about the type of happiness that you can take a picture with and post it on your social networking site. The happiness that I'm talking about cannot be put in your trophy or award room. The happiness I'm talking about cannot fit into an eight by eleven frame. The happiness I'm talking about cannot be put on your refrigerator. The happiness I'm talking about is not in your garage; drive way or outside your home.

The happiness I'm talking about cannot be built on fifty acres of land. The happiness I'm talking about cannot be charged on your credit card. The happiness I'm talking about cannot be put on layaway or found at a thirty percent off sale. The happiness I'm talking about cannot be put around your finger on the left hand. The happiness I'm talking about cannot be obtained by finding "The One" or "Mr. Right" or "Mrs. Right". The happiness I'm talking about cannot be wrapped around your wrist, neck, or inserted in both ear lobes.

This type of happiness does not vary because of your gender. This type of happiness does not vary because of your age. This type of happiness does not vary because of your sexual preference or orientation. This type of happiness does not vary because of your ethnicity. This type of happiness does not vary because of your spirituality. This type of happiness does not vary because of your religion. This type of happiness does not vary because of your employment status. This type of happiness does not vary because of your political affiliations. This type of happiness does not care about whether or not you earn tips, a wage, or a salary. This type of happiness does not care about what type of roof is over your head.

This type of happiness does not care about whether you sleep in a sleeping bag on the street or in a king size bed. This type of happiness does not care about whether you live in a gated community or row housing. This type of happiness does not care about what level of education you have. This type of happiness does not care about your marital status. This type of happiness does not care about your credit score or financial security. This type of happiness does not care about your time-shares.

The happiness I'm talking about is the kind you wake up to. Not wake up and roll over to; I'm not talking about that kind of happiness. I'm talking about the type of happiness when every aspect of your being unifies as one and you wake up. I'm talking about the type of happiness that's yours for life. I'm talking about the type of happiness where you realize that you had it all along, but you were asleep to it. I'm talking about the type of happiness that is so powerful that it flows through you and into other people.

I'm talking about the type of happiness that shines brighter than any diamond known to mankind. I'm talking about the type of happiness that no one can take from you. I'm talking about the type of happiness that's with you no matter what you go through: emotionally, intellectually, physically (Including medically) because it is a part of your **SPIRIT**. This type of happiness is "Outside-the-Box of Society"; this is the type of happiness you experience when you are awake.

There are some people who believe happiness is a way of life. These types of people acknowledge that happiness is an emotion, but they also understand that happiness is a part of their lives. When it comes to relationships these people have happiness at their foundations. One of the major differences with these people that have foundational happiness is that they do not need to depend on someone else to make them happy. Their individual happiness is beneath the surface at the foundation. These types of people constantly have happiness in their lives; the everlasting happiness is a part of their foundation. The second major difference is that these types of people want to share his or her happiness. Therefore, they're not compatible with someone that depends on him or her to make them happy.

Personally, I believe that happiness is an emotion and I still have happiness a part of my foundation. My perspective of life consistently keeps my happiness meter full. Beneath the surface my happiness meter stays full due to: learning the lessons that life has to teach me, the fact that I learn at least three new random things a day, and my sense of humor. I'm constantly learning something new and I do not care if I make mistakes in order for me to learn. Anyone who knows me understands that I have one crazy sense of humor. I find joy in making someone laugh or smile, especially if he or she is having rough day. Since the economy is in such a bad shape, I'm always able to make someone laugh! I love to laugh and often make myself laugh too. I know the horse is almost dead, but do you see why it is important to have an individual foundation?

One of the questions that I often ask on dates is "What does a man have to do to make and keep you happy?" This is a trick question. I'm not about games; however, "Society" has brainwashed women into believing they need a man. So this question allows me to enlighten women, but when I tried it in the past, women did not understand. After this book, I know for a fact that women will understand. Whenever a woman answers the question with, "A man has to..." she has already answered the question wrong. I shouldn't have to do anything to make/keep a woman happy.

A person should be individually happy prior to meeting someone else. When two people are individually happy, they can share their happiness with each other. As opposed to someone depending on you to make him or her happy. Try not to misinterpret my words, when I do little things to bring joy in a woman's life it is because I want to do it. I just do not believe that a man or woman should depend on someone to make him or her happy.

I think people depend on someone to make him or her happy because they have not defined what happiness means to them as individuals. Whenever I ask women for their definitions of happiness many of them have told me that nobody had ever asked them that before. Or people may actually believe it is someone else's duty to make him or her happy because of society's input on happiness and relationships. Once again this goes back to the basics of someone being a part of your life vs. someone being your life. If there is a requirement to make someone happy, then the relationship has been downgraded to a job.

Think about it like this, if a woman depends on me to make her happy, then we are not sharing happiness are we? No one can share happiness if one depends on someone else to make him or her happy. If you are curious if your significant other depends on you to make him or her happy, ask for his or her definition of happiness. If you have to ask that question, you might as well ask yourself what you feel the relationship is built on. As well as asking your significant other what he or she feels the relationship is built on.

Remember a relationship is about sharing, would you rather share your happiness or depend on someone to make you happy? Within my conversations with people I often hear "I can't wait to find someone that can give me that long-term happiness." If you have foundational happiness, then you have long-term happiness. It's very simple.

I know this chapter is supposed to be about happiness, but I want to briefly touch on dependency in relationships. When it comes to dependency in relationships there are two types. The first type of dependency deals with task that needs to be accomplished. For example, your significant other may depend on you to pick him or her up from the airport. If you live with your significant other, he or she may depend on you to pay your share of the bills. The second type of dependency is what I refer to as the "Unhealthy dependencies".

For instance, when a person depends on his or her significant other to: make him or her happy, cure him or her of being lonely, show him or her attention, make him or her feel secure; just to name a few. The second type of dependency is what some men and women use as guides to determine the authenticity of a relationship. Scrap that mindset immediately; your individual foundation determines authenticity. You cannot fake a connection beneath the surface.

Anyways, one day I was at a bookstore looking for an interesting book to read and I bumped into a woman by the name of Chloe. After apologizing to her several times for texting and walking, I noticed the book that was in her hand was one that I read before. So we started talking about the author and the other books that he had written. Next thing you know that topic led to another topic and fifteen minutes flew by. So Chloe and I exchanged numbers and went back to browsing. Approximately a week later, we decided to meet up at a café'.

What I found interesting about Chloe was how much chemistry we had. It was Chloe that validated my theory on "Surface vs. Foundation" in relationships. She was the one that demonstrated to me that I wasn't the only one to perceive relationships in the manner that I do. Our conversation during our first date went straight to the foundation for the both of us. I asked her one of my foundational questions, "What does a man need to do to make/keep you happy?" Chloe replied, "Nothing", which is the correct answer to that question. She racked up a lot of points with that answer.

So I moved on to my next foundational question, "What's your definition of happiness?" She said, "My happiness flows through my relationship with God, so I'm always happy." Chloe's definition of happiness and my definition of happiness are not word-for- word the same. However, her definition of happiness is at her foundation; meaning nothing will ever change the happiness that she has in her life. When you compare foundational happiness to surface happiness there is a distinct difference. Foundational happiness is always with you; it does not matter if you change careers, change your relationship status, etc.

Surface happiness is the immediate gratification from something that makes you "Happy" and is the emotion of being happy. When it comes to this level everything depends on the emotions of you being happy. The question is, when you have not reached your goal to be happy through whichever means you choose; does that mean you're not happy in the moment? If you're not happy in the moment, do you believe that you need a man or woman to make you happy until you reach your goal to be happy? Or is finding a man or woman to make you happy your goal? This level of happiness always takes the form of: "When I meet 'the one' I'll be happy" or "Is there someone that can make me happy?" or "When I meet the man or woman of my dreams; I know I'll be happy." The real question to ask those that believe in this level of happiness is, "What's stopping you from developing your individual happiness at your foundation?"

You are what is stopping you by believing that you need a man or woman to be happy in your life. So what brings happiness into your life? What makes you internally happy at your foundation?

Surface happiness can also take the form of materialistic possessions. There are a lot of people in society that believe in money buying happiness.

These types of people love making money so they can afford the "Finer" things in life that will make them happy. The problem here is that these people are never completely happy. Once they obtain the thing that brings them the happiness-emotion; they want more.

Which really makes sense because the "Happy emotion" does not last forever, unless it is renewed. The only way to renew the emotion is through purchasing more of the "Finer" things in life. As you can probably see, this cycle will continue until the money runs out or they have an unexpected change in their life. What happens when these types of people have a significant decrease in their wage or salaries? They no longer have the ability to enjoy the "Finer" things in life. Logically speaking, these people can no longer afford their happiness, unless they have a credit card. Knowing the different levels of happiness helps you to determine compatibility with another person. **The last thing you want in your life is to be in a relationship with different definitions of happiness.** Hypothetically speaking:

Ex.1 Say you're in a relationship and you do or do not live with your significant other. Your happiness is at your foundation and your significant other has happiness through materialistic possessions. If your significant other is unable to obtain his or her materialistic goals due to a change in career or job, how does that affect your relationship?

Ex. 2 Say you're in a relationship and you do or

do not live with your significant other. Your happiness is right on the surface as well as your significant other's happiness too. The both of you are unable to achieve your materialistic goals. How does this affect your relationship?

In example one, your relationship with your significant other is affected because he or she is no longer happy. So what usually happens? You try to find ways to make your significant other happy; however, since he or she is happy only through materialistic possessions you end up having to buy him or her things. So now the focus of the relationship is how you can make your significant other happy. If you cannot make the other person happy, what happens? The relationship ends because you couldn't make the other person happy. Confusing?

In example two, there are two people who are unhappy in their relationship. So now the both of you are tasked with trying to make the other person happy. Once again, the both of you must buy the other person things in order to make him or her happy. If you cannot afford something, then the other person believes that you cannot make him or her happy and the relationship is over!!

Deep Level of Happiness (Foundational Happiness)= Long-term happiness is "Shared" in the relationship.

Surface Level of Happiness (Shallow Happiness)= Short-term happiness is "Needed" in the relationship.

Chapter 7. Purpose Built

Hopefully, up to this point you understand that one of the principles of life is learning. Some of us have gotten to the point that we no longer care about relationships. Which is partly brought on by dealing with repetitive experiences. Specifically the type of experiences that constantly puts us in a heart broken and/or confused state.

What I find interesting about repetitive experiences (Relationships) is once we shift our perspective we can see a lesson within the experience. Sometimes we have repetitive experiences (Relationships) because we failed to learn the lesson the first time. We thought we learned, (first aspect of learning-emotional response) but we really didn't learn the lesson that is beneath the surface (second aspect of learning). Remember the first aspect of learning is right on the surface and it is based upon the emotional response to an experience.

Anyways, sometimes the repetitive experiences may be necessary to help another person learn what he or she needs to learn. We tend to think that we are the only focus when confronted with an experience when in fact there could be a dual purpose (Two People) for the experience happening. Take cheating for example, if we get cheated on, then we think we are the only focus. So we focus on what lessons that we can learn.

However, by you being the "Victim" of a cheater, you are also a learning lesson for the person that cheated on you. The person who cheated on you may reflect on the "Cheating experience" down the road and learning something about him or herself. I'm in no way shape or form advocating cheating. I'm stating that just because we have the perception through our eyes and we learn; learning can still occur through your life for the other person.

Then there are those experiences that happen for one purpose (A greater purpose) and one purpose only, but because of our "One Track Mind" we keep the pursuit expecting things to pick up where they left off. In other words, we get "Tunnel Vision" on being with an individual and a person becomes the light at the end of the tunnel. Then at that point the emotions go out of control and we tell ourselves along the lines of "I'm never pursing anyone else again, or if someone is interested they have to pursue me..." In our minds that's what we call rejection, in actuality its ignorance. Ignorance in the sense of a greater purpose for that experience, and for the direction that we thought the experience was supposed to go. When we let our emotions take over, they blind us from what we could've learned from that experience. Thus, perpetuating the same cycle of repetitive relationships.

I'm really starting to understand how life operates and how we are all interconnected. Yeah, I know that statement may be bit out there for some left-side dominant individuals specifically, those with the Ph.D's in Psychology. I have noticed that our relationships are not just for companionship, intimacy, and love but also for comfort, and to help us to grow. Sometimes being in a relationship with someone else may be to help us heal from an old internal wound. Sometimes we have experiences that we go through so we can comfort someone else later in life.

Meaning you may find yourself caught up in an experience wondering why it happened to you and the answer may be revealed later in life. It's like on the far end of the spectrum, there could be a person who is going through a similar experience. You may find yourself crossing paths with that person and since you went through the experience, you would be the perfect individual to help comfort that person; you would be the answer to someone's prayers. We are all connected.

Or you could be the individual who is

holding on to a burden for years and that burden is destroying everything within your one-arm reach; metaphorically speaking. The burden is eating you up internally and the way you may start the process to release it, is through being in a relationship. In a way "God" has our backs and will purposely have someone cross our path's to aid in the release of the burden.

That person's only purpose might have been to be with you for a short time, be a shoulder for you, or bring some joy to your life. But some of us have been asleep inside the box so long we cannot possibly make sense to any of that. Our experiences serve as our lessons and have even a greater impact on others. However, when your emotions are out of control, it is impossible to see this perspective.

There are a few of us out there who have gone through some experiences that weigh heavily on our emotions. When we go through these times we ask questions along these lines: "Why me" or "Why am I alone" or "Why does...always happen to me?" When we are at this point its like we are in a hole while it is raining on us and we cannot grip the sides of the hole to climb out. Then a little time will pass and someone will kneel down outside the hole, reach his or her arm out and say, "Do you need some help"? How do we reply to that question? "No, I don't need your help. You don't know what I've been through. You weren't there. Just leave me alone." Then we will go right back to, "I have no one here; I'm all alone. Why do I have to deal with this by myself." Catch my drift?

Sometimes when we pray or "Ask the universe for assistance" and God sends someone to us just to listen and comfort us. Literally an answer to your prayers, but we get wrapped around the axle on the small details like "You weren't there, you do not understand what I been through". And then some of us have the nerve to blame God for not answering our prayers. It is a viscous cycle that needs to be broken. It is hard for God/higher power/universal energy/etc to answer our prayers when we get in our own way.

During those tough times in our lives we may speak out loud or in our heads about our problems. Some people refer to this as prayer or some refer to it as asking the universe for assistance, etc. Personally, it doesn't matter what label you want to apply to it; it doesn't change the outcome. By now you should have noticed that I'm not big on labels or anything that "Society" likes to put in a box. In this case, you asked for help, but refused the help when it got there. Then went right back to wondering "Why" you're alone. Your prayers are heard and responded to prior to the words leaving your mouth. Does that sound a bit odd to you? When we talk to other people about our past relationships we usually get one or both of these statements: "People have seasons" or "Everything happens for a reason".

My father used to tell me all the time that "People have seasons" and "Everything happens for a reason", whenever I told him about the women I dated. I believe in both of the statements even though they are incomplete statements. The complete version includes us having to realize what was the purpose for a person's season and what was the reason for him or her entering/exiting our lives. It is at the self-realization point, when a person truly understands why a person crossed his or her path.

When we understand why a person crossed our path we are better able to shift our perspective on our experiences with that person, of course after our emotions are addressed. If we do not figure out what someone's purpose is, then we will miss out on the learning lesson. Most likely we will repeat the lesson with the same person or with a different person.

Our experiences are more than just the emotions and time that we invested into the relationships, but also the learning aspect that is usually hidden within the experience. It's like all of our experiences are filled with keys that fit into locks inside of us, and when we learn from our experiences it unlocks a compartment within us. The compartment varies from one person to the next, but a person can expect to learn something new about him or herself and learn about life in general.

Chapter 8. Family Foundation

Our Society is bass-ackwards, especially when it comes to relationships with family. We have a tendency to have relationships with family on a pedestal, especially relationships between parents and children. The relationships between parents and children are no different than any other relationship. We still need the fundamentals just like any other relationship: we definitely need communication, emotional integrity, humility, patience, respect, etc.

Respect is a very interesting quality between parents and children. For some odd reason some of us feel as though respect can only exist " From the bottom, up". Meaning respect only exists from the child to the parent. I'm sorry, but that is not how relationships are established and maintained (One Way). I remember as a child telling my dad that I felt he disrespected me. Do you know what he told me? "I'm your father and you're not going to disrespect me in my house" as he reached for the belt. We know how that story ends.

So let me get this straight "Society", parents are the only ones who can say they've been disrespected? Once again that's not right. Tisk Tisk Tisk. That makes no sense and needs to change as well. To this day there are people who still talk about the effects of slavery still lingering in "Society". Specifically, the African American race; once again it's easy for everyone to point fingers at everyone else but not themselves. So I'll take the honor in doing the pointing for you.

I absolutely cannot stand double standards, especially African American Parents who say and do what they feel and think they are above the law. I do not know if you noticed, but the effects of slavery are in parenting as well.

So all of the African American Parents (Including my Parents) pay close attention to the lesson I'm about to teach you. I'm only going through this once. After this period of instruction, I'm confident that you all will understand what the word "Respect" means and how to utilize it within your relationships with your children. The overall learning objective is that you all will know what "Mutual Respect" means and see where your mistakes are. I would say it's common sense, but if it were I would not be explaining. In the three scenes below, you will notice that the children are not disrespectful, but for some odd reason, African American Parents seem to think so. Maybe it's all that built up rage from being oppressed for over 300 years. But, what do I know? I do not have a Ph. D in African American Studies. All I have is a high diploma.

So Let's take a closer look, shall we: Pa (Yells at son for no apparent reason)...And action!!!!

Boy: Yessa em, I showl is sorry, Iz dont knowz whatz iz did

Boy: (Is completely lost)

Pa: You don't need to know, I'm your father, I pay the bills around here. Stop trying to know it all!

Boy: (Is still completely lost)

Boy: (Still respects his Pa): Yessem pa I tries my bestsss nots to dizpoints you.

Pa: Now go do your homework

Boy: Yess em saah

Cut...End Scene....Set up for the next set. I just got up from the floor (I was literally

ROFLOL)...Author(me) (Clears Throat) (Gets Serious) Maybe that example was a bit over "The Line"...Nah! I need to prove my point. Let me give you another example African American parents, don't leave yet there's more:

Ma: (Disrespects Child)...And Action!!!!!

Ma: (Yells through house): Tina

Tina: yes, mom

Ma: Tina get your *** in here and clean this filthy ******* kitchen. Didn't I te Didn't I te Didn't I tell you to clean the*******kitchen before I got home from work today? Didn't I? (Voice escalates) Didn't I? (Walks in kitchen, slams plates around) I tell you to do one *******thing and your fat***can't even do it. I bet your*** can eat a jelly donut though.

Tina: I'm sorry mom I forgot (Ma takes her hand wraps it around Tina's cheeks/jaw)

Ma: Roll your eyes at me if you want to

Tina: I didn't roll my eyes, ma

Ma: So you want to talk back to me now.... huh? I'll knock you into the middle of next week (or the infamous I'll hit you so hard, you'll think lightening struck you)

Ma: (Pulls Switch from purse)... Cut.... End Scene...Good work everyone. Maybe the light bulb still hasn't gone off yet. This is the last example; if you don't get it now, then maybe you should lower your pride level and raise your humility level. For some odd reason, parents think they cannot learn from their children. Lets continue:

Set the scene.... And Action!!!

Dad: (Arrives home from work, to see bicycle in the front yard)

Kevin: (Opens front door to go outside)

Dad: Kevin, how many times have I told you about your bike?

Kevin: (Proceeds to move bicycle around to the back of the house)

Dad: Don't walk away from me boy when I'm talking to you.

Kevin: I was tr (Dad Slaps Kevin across the face) {Kevin was attempting to say, "I was trying to move the bicycle"}

Dad: Don't talk back to me; you may get away with that **** with your mama, but not me. You need some******discipline. Soft***kids. The kids today I'll tell ya. Phew

Kevin: (Starts Crying)

Dad: Stop crying. Grow the **** up; stop being a girl. Hold your head up high; stick your chest out, men don't cry.

Kevin: (Sniffles, Wipes tears from eyes) Yes sir.

Cut...End Scene. Great job everyone. You can go home for the day.

Is it just me or does this relationship remind you of slavery? You know, the master always treats the child I mean slave with disrespect and instills fear for control? You know what I mean right? No matter how bad the Master treats the slave, the slave must always be obedient and respectful. Oh, and the slave must never question the master because the master knows what's best for the slave. For the slave to question the master is disrespectful and is automatic grounds for verbal and physical abuse. You know you must keep that slave inline; for they know not what is best for them.

Oh, and if the slave rebels then the Master wonders why and talks it over with other parents, I meant Slave owners. The parents, I mean slave owners talk about how they treat their children, I mean slaves a lot better than other Slave owners. These parents raise their children through fear, but call it Love. And wonder why their children grow up in fear and not enough Love. Hmm, I wonder why. The slave mentality that lingers in "Society" has always been present within the parenting styles of the majority of African American or black parents, as well as within other nationalities or demographics. But like I said it's way easier to look at everyone else with a magnifying glass compared to looking at the person in the mirror.

Any Questions, comments, concerns, complaints? Congratulations, you have passed your first official course in "Mutual Respect". I wish you the very best with your children. Class

Dismissed!!!

Moving On...

Respect is a two-way street; children should respect their parents and parents should respect their children. Once again "Society" is a bit lost. The only time parents' talk about respect being a two-way street is when the children are over 18 and that is IF a child has brought up "Mutual Respect". Parents believe a two-way street does not exist when the children are below 18. That as well needs to change. Brothers should respect their sisters and sisters should respect their brothers; brothers should respect brothers and sisters should respect sisters. Simple?

Guess what?

The relationships between parents and

children are built on a strong foundation just like any other relationship. If there is no foundation then you are left with only one thing, the biological connection. You have probably heard this before: "She may be my mother, but she is not a mom" or "He may be my father, but he is not a dad" or "He may be a sibling, but he is not my brother" or "She may be a sibling, but she is not my sister".

These statements are not mean or disrespectful, what people are simply saying is, "I'm connected to my parents biologically, but there is no relationship" or "I'm connected to my siblings biologically, but there is no relationship. A biological connection is **not** an automatic relationship creator; there is no easy way out, it is called building. So how about parents and children start building for a change, instead of just going with the flow of bass-ackwards "Society". Parents need to get that through their "Slave-Mentality" heads real quick because there are children who are real close to snapping, if they haven't already.

Now, the three scenes are not just for African American Parents; I'm "African American" (I'll get into why I used the quotes in the last chapter) and dealt with that type of ignorance as a kid, and it needs to stop. In fact how about all parents no matter the race stop and ask themselves (If it pertains to you), "Why did I think I could do that to my children and see nothing wrong with it? When you get that answer, I would love to know why. So hopefully this lesson on mutual respect will allow a more loving relationship between parents and children.

We all know that there is no manual to be a perfect parent; people publish "How to" be the best parent type of books, but they do not work. Also, there are no manuals to be a perfect child or to be a perfect sibling. I do not need to be a parent to understand about being a parent. Parents do the best that they can just like children and siblings; however, they still need to possess humility and integrity when questioning themselves about their relationship with their children. I do not know if you have noticed the inner cycle within parenting exist outside of parents.

It is the cycle of learning and applying. When our parents were children they said, "When I have children I will not do...." or "When I have children I will do..." In fact, there are children probably saying those exact same words right now. Parenthood is all about learning, teaching, and preparing children to survive on their own. It really is that simple. I do not need to write a 50-page chapter on parenting. But what do I know. I do not have a Ph. D in Family Counseling. Do you have "Mutual Respect" with your children/parents?

Chapter 9. Different Foundations

We live in a society that has a lot influence on our individual lives. It's like before we are born "Society" hands every parent expecting a newborn, a sheet with "Life's Directions" on it. Along with a pocket size compass attached just in case we get lost. Not too long ago I reached a point in my life where I decided to take the "Directions" with the compass and chuck them as far away from me as possible. I immediately turned to the opposite direction of where "Society" thought I should go, and decided to create my own path.

Did I know where I was going? Not a clue, but I much rather have found out along the way than to follow "Society's Directions" just because we've been doing it two hundred plus years. While I was walking creating my own path, I started to notice the farther I got away from "Society" the more I was beginning to change. My perception of life was not just zoomed in through my eyes; I was able to zoom out and see life as a whole. So I continued to walk and I noticed that I didn't have one single thought on my mind. For once in my life my mind was calm...still.

While I was walking I realized that my observations of life had changed as well. When I turned around to look back at "Society" I noticed that it became very difficult to see life. I started to notice that there seemed to be more darkness hovering over life than there was light passing through. So I stopped walking and sat down for a bit. I started thinking about the darkness and the light and two words popped into my head, fear and love. There is more fear in our world than there is love. I began asking myself, "How could there be more fear than love?" I stood up and continued walking even farther from society. While I was walking I said to myself, "Maybe it's because of our actions".

Again I stopped walking and sat down for bit. Another thought popped into my head, "It's not just our actions, it's our thoughts. Our thoughts cause our actions. An individual has the power to take one thought and create reality. It is like that one thought sends a message to every aspect of your being to come together to help you create your thought. It hit me; we create fear; we create the darkness that hovers over our world.

There is an overwhelming amount of fear and not enough love. The absence of fear leaves us with love. Love is all there is. Compassion, humility, integrity, patience, friendship, etc; all comes down to love.

The mind is where fear is created; love is a part of our spirit, which happens to connect us to each other and the universe. The spirit is nothing more than energy; in fact it's the energy that triggers our tears to form and roll down our cheeks. Hate, anger, pride, apathy, worry, all boils down to fear; we create it. Instead of using the mind to assist in spreading more love, we use the mind to create fear. FEAR that holds us back as individuals and as mankind from living to our full potential. FULL, meaning our rational mind, emotions, and spirit working as one to spread more love.

Instead of how it is now, where the inside of a person is a battlefield. When a person zooms out he or she will see our world is a battlefield as well. Could there possibly, maybe, perhaps, kind of, be some sort of a connection? "Society" manipulates people by instilling fear to create power and control to ultimately create a box. This box was created thousand's and thousand's of years ago and to this day the box is still present. I don't know if you've noticed but a lot of our greatest ideas throughout our world history have been "Outside the box". I "think" outside the box and I live outside the box.

When you move outside the box, you really began to notice that fear is only generated for those inside the box and love is all there is. It took for me to abandon "Society's-Life Script", to see all of this. "We are our own worst enemy", I'm sure you've heard that before. This statement doesn't just apply to us as individuals, but us as a whole, us as mankind. People look at our environment, Global-warming, etc and say, "God's angry" and comments along those lines. Once again we created it. God is love. When you're inside the box, you're asleep, and you think God is above you. When you're outside the box, you're awake, and you know you and God are one.

Society is tunnel vision on actions alone, but it's the thoughts that cause the actions. Each thought that we form projects itself into the universe in the form of energy. Our thoughts hold the same amount of energy as our actions do. "It's the thought that matters", I'm sure you heard this statement before. Matter is energy; thus, thoughts are energy. But what do I know; I don't have a Ph. D in Physics. We as mankind and individuals must stop the thoughts and actions of fear or we will end up destroying our planet. I challenge you, the individual, the reader, and the possible critic, to monitor your thoughts for 24 hours.

Better yet, do it for 12 hours. Right down whatever thoughts cross your mind no matter what they are. Then grab a blank sheet of paper, create two columns, and label one side fear and the other love. Count the number of thoughts that were based on fear and do the same for love. Record the totals for each category. When you have the totals, look at them and then monitor your thoughts again.

What I wrote about in this book can be applied to our lives outside of just relationships. The main purpose for finally finishing this book is for people to learn from their experiences, by acknowledging our connection to them and addressing our emotions. When we do that we really began to understand why we are here.

Hopefully more people will understand that there is a higher purpose for our lives. Personally, there seems to be an inner battle when it comes to the higher purpose. When you know your higher purpose or real purpose for being here, you feel it and just know. However, once again, our rational mind wants to know why and starts assessing our abilities to figure out how we can fulfill the purpose. Unfortunately, that part of our being is overstepping its boundaries. This is when the spiritual side of us takes over. Which is another reason why having a strong self-relationship (Foundation) is important.

As far as the purpose goes, there is no purpose that is more important than another purpose. The "Big Picture" or common theme of a "Higher Purpose" is to learn and serve. Whether you're a: parent, educator, news anchor, chef, member of the armed forces, police officer, accountant, CEO, convenient store cashier, secretary, babysitter, financial advisor, medical professional, religious/spiritual leader, counselor, psychologist, politician, dentist, mechanic, street sweeper, author, music artist, writer, painter, sculptor, actor, professional athlete, fire fighter, etc we are all here to serve.

No matter how egotistical or selfish a person is in any of the examples above, they are all still in a position to serve others and learn. Painters serve others by utilizing illustrations to express a different perspective. People find solace in music whether there are lyrics or no lyrics. The ones with lyrics may provide a shared emotion or a shared perspective of life. Music without lyrics seems to speak to and soothe the spirit. Professional athletes not only entertain, but they also inspire.

The higher purpose is not something to distinguish you from everyone else. It's not ego-based; it's the real purpose for our lives. There are two purposes. The first purpose is what we "Think" (Rational Mind) we should be doing and the other is what we "Feel" (Spirit) we should be doing. I FELT like I should write this book. The learning is a part of our purpose for being here on earth. If we were all "Perfect" we wouldn't be here because we would know everything. The learning is what prepares our lives for that higher purpose and a peaceful mind. The peaceful mind enables us to carry out our real purpose without fear. **People say that without fear the sky is the limit; well without fear, the sky is your playground.**

The lessons come in all shapes and sizes. Learning from an experience doesn't always have to take the form of some "Extraordinary event". In which the clouds part, the sunset's, we feel a whisk breeze, and we get an "Aha" moment. Learning occurs: in our day-to-day conversations, within our relationships (Types are irrelevant); at our jobs/careers; talking to a stranger; walking down the street; reading; listening to music; during our chores; and pretty much everything within our individual lives.

I chose to focus on relationships because within the market there aren't any books that focus on the individual in clear non-technical language. At one point in our lives, we've heard someone say "Focus on you", but nobody has never really explained how to do so. Instead, the majority of books rather focus on generalizing men and women. Unless someone has dated every man or woman on this earth, then he or she can't speak on all men or women.

Think about this, how can randomly selecting men and women to interview, end up representing all men and women on the planet? And the majority of the people conducting these interviews have Ph. D's. Does that make any sense? Even if someone did date everyone, we are all individuals. Individuals may have similarities but there is no person who is 100% identical to another person. But I forgot for a moment there, that society enjoys placing everything inside a box.

Everything that I've written is applicable to: both genders, any sexual preference/orientation, those with different socio-economic backgrounds, all ages, all nationalities, all demographics, and those that have religious and/or spiritual beliefs. In other words, it's applicable to individuals; with individuals there are no labels.

Some people (Men & Women) are confused about relationships. They think that if they're lonely they need to find a relationship. Some think that if they are insecure, they need to find someone who can make them secure. Some think that if they are not happy, they need to find someone that can make them happy. It's like whatever a person doesn't have or whatever a person is missing they think they need a relationship to fill the void. All you need is yourself.

One of the problems that I've noticed is that people enter into a relationship with the "Need Mindset" and expectations of a "Sharing Relationship." Having a "Need" mindset and "Sharing" expectations are complete opposites of each other; which is one of the many reasons why I know people run into a lot of issues. Wouldn't you rather share your life with someone?

Wouldn't you rather share your perception of life with someone? Wouldn't you rather share your uniqueness? Wouldn't you like to share your life lessons with someone? Wouldn't you like to share your wisdom from your learning lessons?

The thing is, you cannot share what you are oblivious to. So building your foundation and making the connection beneath the surface gives you the ability to share your life. You can share the mental, intellectual, emotional, and spiritual aspects of your individual lives. And that's what I feel people would like to have in a relationship. We are consistently learning and each learning lesson helps us to grow in the above categories. Wouldn't you rather grow together in relationship with someone? Where you can grow through your significant other, while growing through your own life.

Now, I'm not some person sitting up high looking down on everyone. I'm still learning about life like everyone else, I just have a different perspective on life and living. I still get frustrated like the next person; to this day I have no clue why people wait until they are twenty feet in front of your car, before they decide to dash across the road.

Throughout the book I refer to the experiences that we've faced as "Positive and Negative Experiences". Our emotions play a key role in what we learn from an experience and how we perceive an experience. Let's take a "Negative" experience for instance. If I do not address my emotions and let my emotions fly, then it's labeled a "Negative experience."

However, with that same experience if I address my emotions and learn from the experience is it still considered a "Negative experience"? Or is the experience a "Negative experience with benefits"? Or is it called a full-blown positive experience?

Our perception of life depends on how we perceive our experiences, which are based on our emotional response. Either way it seems like life is the teacher and we are the students. I don't think the teacher cares what we call the lessons as long as we learn the lesson. If you fail and learn from failing, are you still a failure or are you successful? What is failure? What is success?

Each day that I live, I learn something new. Our lives are more than just: finding that special person, finding that career, financial security, and having a family. I'm a firm believer that our lives are about learning the lessons that life has to teach us.

Each individual has his or her own set of lessons that they need to learn; that's why it makes no sense to bother yourself with comparing yourself to someone else. Our emotions and perception of the lessons, determine if we learn or not. If we do not learn, then we repeat the same lesson until learning occurs. No different than the process in academia; if we learn we pass, if we fail we repeat. If we fail a class, course, or an academic term, then we do not move on. Once again the concept is transferable to other aspects of life, if you wake up and can hop outside the box.

I live my life with no regrets. To regret an experience is to erase every learning lesson between that experience and the present time. Since all of our experiences are full of learning lessons, how is it possible to have regrets? Those that have regrets are not familiar with the lessons within his or her experiences. Do you have any regrets?

One of the key concepts throughout this book is about perception and how it plays a large role within our lives. People can learn a lot from just observations, you don't even need to speak. The only time you may need to speak is to question what you saw or heard. I'm not saying people need to convert to how I see life, but I feel that people could use another lens for theirs. Everything that I've discussed is a few of the lessons that I've learned in life, and that I'm continuing to learn as I continue to live.

Several times throughout my life I've always heard people say, "Knowledge is Power", but I think it's an inaccurate statement. Think about it, how is knowledge powerful if it is just kept in a box and not let free? Knowledge is powerful when it's applied; when it's applied it converts into wisdom. When the wisdom can be shared with others is when it is empowering. Knowledge without application is powerless. Wisdom is power, not knowledge.

Throughout the book, you've probably noticed that I'm always making reference to society. I don't question society to be difficult; I question society because all of the things we do and say make no sense. People have become puppets and only "Move" based on what society says. When people stay "Inside the box" of

"Society" they only see what's directly in front of them or behind them. People end up chasing after what "Society" says they need. People chase happiness but can't define it. I really think people should "Re-define" their lives by asking questions. Seek answers not only with your rational mind, but also with your spirit. You maintain a balance between the mind and spirit; you maintain a balance in life.

I refuse to perpetuate the cycle of ignorance within the various aspects of "Society". Wait a second doesn't the "N- word" mean ignorant? This book is full of me showing how ignorant "Society" is (US); particularly our Nation's Leader's with the Advanced-Ivy League College Degree's (Ph. D's in specific fields of study). Lets do a logic problem real quick. If N-word is to ignorant; ignorant is to society, what is Society? Ignorance means without education and/or knowledge. What does this book tell you about the educational system? The educational system is based off of knowledge; I've dismantled and crushed the knowledge. Answer: the educational system is non-existent.

I refuse to refer to myself as Black or

respond to someone who calls me black. I will no longer fill in any more forms where the choices are "Black" or "African American" including the Census, so I suggest the U.S. get started on that quickly. My skin tone is brown and my facial/body hair is black; two distinctive colors. How can the US move pass race if we cannot even get the colors right? I guess that is too simple right. But what do I know? All I have is a high school diploma. From now on all people who were formerly called "Black" will be "Brown"; the "N-word" refers to a black person; which does not exist anymore/never did.... Now we can resign the NAACP because I just took care of that for all of us.

On that note, "Society's-Logic", is a new oxymoron that I put into existence today to replace the word "Mature" because my new word actually makes sense. Wow, all that with a high school diploma. I refuse to not accept responsibility for my emotions because "I'm only human." I refuse to believe I can't be objective; when I address my emotions and shift my perspective I can be objective. I refuse to live my life aimlessly without observations. I refuse to believe that I can only learn about life within four walls and a chalkboard in front of me.

I refuse to believe wisdom has anything to do with age or "Living longer"; wisdom has to do with learning and applying. I refuse to believe I can only think outside the box in an academic environment. I refuse to believe that I need a formal education to define my life; my perception of life, the drive of my spirit and my learning lessons define my life. I refuse to believe that money buys happiness.

I refuse to do what everyone else does just because. I much rather stand by myself (Like I do now) for something I believe in, than follow the majority because everyone is doing it. I refuse to believe women and "Mothers" are the only ones who have a strong intuition and listen to their intuition. Intuition comes from spirit; spirit knows no labels or parameters and definitely not genders! I refuse to believe our children need to be medicated because of their abstract thought (Outside the Box to the fiftieth exponent); creativity, and imagination; I would not be able to write this without all three.

Being different scares "Society". Instead of changing the systems "Society" rather change our children, which once again is "Bass-Ackwards". I refuse to believe the so-called "Learning disabilities" are disabilities. They are only disabilities to those who live "Inside the Box"; "Outside the Box" they are gifts. I refuse to believe in "Who does something for nothing" statement. When I do something for someone it's because I want to do it and it's as simple as that. I refuse to believe there is even a choice between Integrity and Loyalty; Integrity wins every single time. I don't care if you are family or not. I refuse to believe that our political system even exists.

Hypothetically speaking, say I'm following the Presidential campaign and I feel that the individual representing the Republican Party has the best interest for me. However, my mother happens to rely on social programs and/or government assistance, which happens to fall under the Democratic Party. If I cast my vote for the Republican candidate I'm ultimately saying, my well-being is more important than my mother's well being. I cannot in a clear conscience choose between two parties. I refuse to perpetuate the cycle of choosing between "2 evils".

In other words, for the slow individuals (Politicians), I'm not voting until the system changes. If the political system is all about the people, then why do people find themselves in these types of predicaments? Why do I have to choose between my life and someone else's life that I value? Hmmm isn't the Republican Party about morals and values? There goes that word value again. Could there maybe, possibly, kind of, sort of, be a contradiction within the U.S. Political System?

Our country has strayed so far from "...the government of the people, by the people, and for the people..." If you're a Politician and a bit confused about that quote, it's from the Gettysburg Address. You know Abraham Lincoln, our 16th President, still not ringing a bell? Perhaps, that over-priced education and power is more appealing than remembering our history. But what do I know, I don't have a Ph. D in

History all I have is a high school diploma. According to our political system voting doesn't equal change it equals temporary fix, if you can even call it that. Our political system is like some medical doctors; they treat the symptoms but have not the slightest clue on what caused the symptoms. I'm a very simple person. I like to keep things very very simple so everyone can keep up.

So I'll break this down "Barney Style" for the possible Politician reading my words right now. The US is full of red (Republican) and blue (Democrat) states. When a Republican is in the office (Presidency), the Democrat's are left out. When a Democrat is in the office, the Republican's are left out. Are you still following me Mr. or Mrs. Politician? How about a President who actually represents the United States of America? Not the United Democrat States of America. Not the United Republican States of America. But the United...Red...and Blue...States of America, did I go slow enough for you Mr. or Mrs. Politician? We need a balance, having one or the other party in the office doesn't give us a balance. But what do I know? I don't have a Ph. D in Political Science. All I have is my high school diploma.

I refuse to believe that life's concepts can only be applied in the experiences in which we've learned them. All of life's concepts can be used in every aspect of life. I refuse to believe that spirituality can be in a box. I refuse to believe that it's better to be a leader than a follower. Some of the best leaders, once followed, and learned from his or her leader's mistakes. I refuse to believe life is short; death is just unexpected. I've noticed that people make the statement of life being short when someone has died unexpectedly. I refuse to believe that death is the end of life. Death is the end of life in the physical form, but the spirit continues to live. And the most important, I refuse to have my spiritual-self imprisoned by the mind.

Unfortunately, slavery is still very prevalent in society today. The form of slavery that I'm referring to is the individual who is a slave to Master Fear and its associates (Master Need & Master Dependency). Master Need and Master Dependency are children of Master Fear. Master Fear says, "You'll never be anything in life; you'll never have a healthy relationship; you'll never experience love". You listen to Master Fear because of the one time or maybe two times that Master Fear said, "I'm telling you don't do it, he or she is only using you" and Master Fear was right. At that point in your life, you extended your contract with Master Fear.

Once you extended your contract, Master Need said, "Don't worry about anything in life; all you **need** to do is find someone that can take care of you." Then Master Dependency inserted its two cents, "Yeah, all you need to do is **depend** on someone financially and emotionally. And all your problems will be solved." Master Fear and its associates do not want you to step out of your "Bubble" or "Box". Until you break the chains from Master Fear and its associates, you will remain a slave.

Until you cut the string from society, you will remain a puppet. By keeping the chains and strings attached, you will remain "Inside the Box" where society has control. There is barely any light "Inside the Box" and that is not compatible with the spirit; the spirit is meant to shine. When your spirit is inside a box, the spirit definitely can't shine and it makes it extremely difficult to receive any light from God; who is outside the box. Somehow "Society" has managed to put God in a box. You've probably heard this before, "That wasn't God, it was luck" or "God didn't do that, it was a coincidence". To me the word coincidence means purpose. But what do I know? I do not have a Ph. D in English. All I have is my high school diploma.

For those who rely on logic; God works in

mysterious ways, so how is it logical to put a mysterious being, God, in a box, label it and say "This is all God can do"? I read an article not too long ago and it was about a man who fell 47 stories and survived; which defies everything that I learned in Physics. Maybe, um, possibly, um, perhaps, sort of God was trying to send a message. The message is, "Yall can't put me in no box". But what do I know; I don't even have a college degree. All I have is my high school diploma.

Earth is full of polar opposites such as: positive energy-negative energy, up down, male-female, day-night, etc. Why do we refer to God-Creator as a male? You know: "I give thanks to my heavenly father" or "God and his glory". Could there possibly, maybe, sort of, kind of, perhaps be a connection to "Patriarchal Society"? (Rhetorical question)

Maybe it's just me but I would think God would be a combination between male and female; the yin and the yang. I mean we are all (Men & Women) created in God's image right? Religion & Science came together not too long ago and confirmed the "God Particle". Could there maybe, um, possibly, probably, um, perhaps, um, be a purpose for that? But what do I know? I don't have a Doctor of Divinity Degree; All I have is a high school diploma.

When we were born our spirit was free and fearless. As we continued to grow our surroundings had a huge impact on our spirit. The more we were developing intellectually and emotionally, the more some of us became disconnected spiritually. Some of us became unbalanced to the point that our spirit was barely shinning. When fear popped into the picture at young age for a lot of us, our spirit became trapped (No wiggle room). It's very difficult for our light (spirit) to shine when there is darkness (fear) in the way.

When fear is removed entirely, and we restore the balance between the mind and the spirit; we move entirely by the spirit. At this point the spirit can do what it came to do without us getting in the way. The balance allows the spirit to utilize the rational mind, emotions, and physical body as a team. With this type of cohesion there is nothing you can't do. Our light shines brighter than it has ever shined before and we become full of joy. Joy that you have doing the most routine things in your life and joy that you just want to spread with everyone.

The mind can either be a gift to the spirit or a curse to the spirit. The mind can be used to help the spirit flow or help the ego grow. In order for the spirit to flow, you have to let go of the ego. Otherwise you'll be like a dog; chasing it's own tail, going absolutely nowhere.

To think is to know; to not know is to flow.
To flow is not to think. To think is to mind;

No mind is spirit. Spirit is not to think.
Spirit is to flow; mind is to know.
Flow is no mind.

Fear is to mind; mind is to block.
Block is to not flow. Not flow is to fear.
Love is to Spirit; Spirit is to flow.
Flow is no mind. No mind is to Love.

Fear blocks the flow of love

There is so much depth to human beings and even more depth as individuals; yet, some of us live and view our lives right on the surface. And actually expect to find meaning there. People think they can find all their answers on the surface; it's the surface that distracts you from what matters; the place beneath the surface. It's the surface that allows the emotions to cloud our perceptions and makes it complicated for people to shift their perspective. It's the surface that mesmerizes people and leads them through life without a "Perception of Life" or any observations of life.

Nevertheless, the surface will give you a perception of politics or a perception of rap music. Wait a second, isn't politics and rap music a part of life? Some of us can answer questions about politics or rap music, but have difficulty answering, "What's your perception of life?"

The answer to this question influences: your thoughts, choices, decisions, actions, emotional response, religious/spiritual beliefs, how you live your life, etc. "What's your perception of life?" should be a question that's asked from grade school on and not just in America. Your observations of life will give you the answer to the question. Your observations of life are based on your lessons and individual foundation; hence,

"Your" perception of life. You don't need to be in a philosophy club to answer the question nor have a Ph. D in Philosophy.

Don't get me wrong, I'm not against education, I self-educate as you can probably tell; I'm against those who believe what follows after their last name is supposed to mean something to me. I'm against titles and labels that are only found inside and on the box. I'm against those who believe a college degree measures intellect. I'm against those who believe a college degree means they have stopped learning and there is nothing else to learn. I'm against those who judge an individual based on his or her level of formal education. I've learned more about life and myself just from observing life outside of the classroom than inside the classroom.

What irritates me the most about our (US) educational system, specifically college (for now), is that college cost money. If I pay for college, I should learn what I want to learn, not what "Society" believes I "Should" learn. I have broad interests, but I like to get deep within the subjects of my interest. In college they say, "When you graduate you will be well rounded", well rounded on the surface is what I've observed.

You take several different classes just to hit the surface like a ball bouncing on the pavement. And on top of that you graduate owing thousands of dollars. On the other hand, the public library is free and my Internet at home costs me $40 a month. What's sad is I have entered college courses in which I've learned more about topics on my own time than being in the classroom.

For $40 a month I get to explore my curiosities without being limited on how deep I'm allowed to go. I've asked questions in classes and some professors' said I was challenging them. My intent was never to challenge, but to understand and simply get some answers to a few "Why" questions that I asked. I figured since I was in college to learn and the professors had specific fields of study, they could shed some light on a few of my questions.

Apparently, questions aren't supposed to be asked in college and I'm supposed to just sit there and listen. If I'm supposed to just sit there in the classroom and pay $x,xxx for 3 credits; I might as well sit at home, ask questions out loud, find the answers on the internet and pay $40 a month. That's just my opinion though. But what I do know, I don't have a Ph. D in Mathematics. All I have is a high school diploma with an old (2005) SAT score of 810 (combined) and graduated from Centennial High School in Maryland with a 2.31 Grade Point Average.

Everything in life is connected, primarily below the surface. You just have to turn inwards. Even if you have spiritual and/or religious beliefs (Or ways of life), you still have to do your part and learning is a part of us doing our part. I hope that wasn't too confusing. I don't know who started the rumor that we don't have to do anything at all, but just wait. I wonder if it was the same person who said that men aren't emotional and brought the word "Perfect" and "Mature" into existence. I think life is pretty simple and straightforward but we complicate the simplest things. When I read books I see links/connections/concepts/ the **BIGGER PICTURE** and that's the reason why formal **EDUCATION** and me **ARE NOT COMPATIBLE.** When I "think" I see analogies in my head.

Anyone who has ever had a conversation with me knows that I love analogies. For the longest, I just kept thoughts to myself because nobody has ever seen things the way I see them. And when I speak out it just causes friction between everyone (including my family) and myself. It frustrates me when I see people hurting and I know that they caused their own suffering by listening and depending on "Society" for everything. People go to books for answers and the ones that are out, don't have them.

The U.S. attempts to shove education down every ones throat and stating it's the only way to live your life. Since I just proved that a college degree doesn't mean much, how about we redirect the money from the Department of Education to places that actually need the money; just a little suggestion. I know of a few Non-Profit Organizations that could really use the money.

It's impossible for Ph. D's to think outside the box because they are still inside the box. To think outside the box; you actually have to live outside the box. But I guess that makes too much sense right? The Ph. D's and the "Relationship-Experts" think they see the "Big Picture" but they are easily distracted by the smaller pictures, which is so so very sad.

As you can see I don't mind rattling the cage, sometimes the cage needs to be rattled to get some answers and to get people moving with a sense of purpose and direction. Like I said "Society" is bass-ackwards; completely upside down, my mission is to change that and I can't do it by myself. As individuals we have everything we need and the tools to fix everything. I hope these words inspire more people to be individuals and not puppets or slaves.

I hope these words inspire more people to chuck the "Life-Script" and to create their own paths in life. When I woke up, I immediately tore off the chains and cut the strings from "Society". Now, I'm actually able to enjoy and have a healthy life, imagine that. Like I said, "Wisdom is power, not knowledge." I hope my wisdom will be able to help you to learn and grow within your own individual life.

We need more individuals; there is a lot that needs to change in "Society". "Society's" puppets and slaves obviously, have nothing to contribute, but misdirection. I know I may sound a bit random at times, but there is a lot that needs to be said and changed. Like I said, we do a lot of things that make no sense and when you ask people why they do it they don't even know. I still have plenty of other thoughts on other things in "Society" that need to change. I've always been told to be quiet and labeled as disruptive in the US education system for seeking answers. My father telling me I "Need" an education and saying that I'm stubborn. Sorry Pop, I'm not stubborn; I just refuse to do things that make no sense whatsoever.

I'm no longer holding back and I will continue to write and speak my spirit (Not my mind). My mother is the only person who has ever supported my perception of life; at least a few of the thoughts I shared with her. "A mother's Love…" is the only thing "Society" has ever gotten right. So "Society" I thank you for that one and only true statement!

This is who and what I am; people can label me all day long, I'm not here to make friends; I really could care less. I'm living my life for something that's larger than you and me. We are all doing it, but some of us are still asleep inside their comfy little box (I'll be changing that quickly), so I hope you awaken soon, if you're not already awake now.

Now, since I have your undivided attention we can get down to brass tax and the purpose for the encrypted messages. The self-relationship is really your spirit/higher self it connects you with God and everyone else. Fear needs to be removed so you can feel God's light/love. The US is the focus for a lot of the issues that is happening on earth and why we can't move forward with evolution, until we fix a lot of the issues with fear and love. The US is the only country that has its hands in just about every country's cookie jar.

As well as having problems with holding on to things that do not work for the time that we are in now, like the US Constitution, etc; hence why I wrote about: foundational happiness, relationships and perceptions, double standards, parenting, all the I refuse to statements above, and everything that I questioned that you know makes no sense. My perspective (Our new shared perspective) will help us to focus on what matters, which is love.

First of all, everything in the US is based on the educational level and how that is the way for the future. I had to break down the word "Mature", so everyone could understand that having a college degree doesn't mean you know everything in life. A Ph. D stands for Philosophy Degree and Philosophy means Love of wisdom. It doesn't mean that you know everything in a specific field; it means that you Love learning, due to wisdom coming from learning. However, the Ph. D's of "Society" Love misdirection as well. How can you Love misdirection but possess a Ph.

D? Again, what does this tell you about the credibility of Ph. D holder? The Formal educational system is blocking our growth as mankind because of the "Box" of misdirection's it created.

Slavery/parenting chapter was needed to act as a wake up call to the parents that disrespect their children for no reason. I had to use it to further show how a regular person without a degree is still credible. The two purposes from writing all of this is to actually help people and to start the process of taking away the power from the US to use their college degrees to challenge anything spiritually "Outside of the Box". That's why I was adamant about proving that I only had a high school diploma, and not an advanced college degree or even any degree. I was not on some ego-trip with the high school diploma vs. Ph. D, everything I said had a purpose no matter how chaotic or random it may have seemed. The rational mind will never understand the spirit or its plans. The rational mind always wants to know the why's for everything in life. "Society" acts as if the rational mind is a separate entity, but the rational mind is only one aspect of our being.

Secondly, the US Political System is worthless, which makes the people in the U.S. and the rest of the world miserable. Everything is connected remember? It's not the President, Senate, House of Representatives, etc; they are all pawns it's the Political Structure itself. The political structure is based off of the U. S. Constitution.

Thirdly, the U.S. Constitution is based off of

the Bible; specifically, Christianity. Thousands, thousands, and thousands of years ago man needed power. The words that pop into my head about the Bible are "Learning Lessons" and "Love".

However, man needed control so man inserted "Fear" into the Bible. What is the best way to get power (for control)? You get power by instilling fear in everyone's mind. Hence, Prerequisites to Heaven, God's Laws, the devil, hell, etc. God's laws, the devil, hell, etc; do not exist. The "Other Side" is spirit because there is no rational mind to create Fear; Love is all there is on the "Other Side". And turning inwards to connect with spirit is to experience the "Other Side". Our rational mind + the ego + fear+ unaddressed emotions (Causes chaos in our lives)

+ being inside the "Box" of "Society" = "The Devil". In other words, we have a choice to be the "Devil" or not. However, there is some truth to the Anti-Christ, if you can shift your perspective just for a moment. Christ aka Christ Consciousness is higher dimensional energy (9th), which is spirit and is Love. Anti-Christ is anything that has to do with fear, the ego, unaddressed emotions, hate, apathy, pride, everything that is the opposite of Love; hence, Anti-Christ.

In case I lost you; Christ is to Love as Anti-Love is to Anti-Christ. Anti-Christ is to Fear. And Fear is to block the flow of Love. People misinterpreted the Bible. Currently in the world as I've stated and you observed, there is more fear (Anti-Christ energy) than Love (Christ, aka Christ energy aka Christed energy). Earth is currently changing from the 3rd dimension to the 5th dimension. The 5th dimension is what people have commonly known as Heaven. Heaven is in the process of coming to Earth. Which is why and how Christ Consciousness will be received this time around. The last time that Christ (9th dimension) came to Earth (3rd dimension) people misinterpreted the Christ energy as well as used the Bible to instill Fear for control.

Therefore, in revelations of the Bible; when it says something along the lines of Christ returning to destroy the Anti-Christ, it means that Love will destroy Fear, since Fear blocks the flow of Love. Meaning all the systems of "Society" that were built on manipulation, no integrity, fear, the ego etc will be destroyed by Love, so Love can flow freely outside the box!!! Love heals and will heal every being on Earth. Christ energy is accessible to all of us if we allow ourselves to turn inwards to connect with spirit. Spirit is pure Love and God is Love. We all have spirits and all the spirits combined and separate equal God. God is a part of us and we are a part of God. We are one. Being created in God's image means to possess male and female energy; means to possess the ability to create our realities; means to possess the ability to Love all and means the ability to be.

God IS LOVE. LOVE IS THE ANSWER TO ALL OF EARTH'S PROBLEMS. All God has ever wanted to do was give us love. But that dang rational mind (Where fear is created and stored), got in the way. Fear blocks the flow of love within ourselves, to other beings, and to God. All of us; EVERY

SINGLE HUMAN BEING MUST COME TOGETHER AS ONE AND WITH LOVE. The irony here is Education and Christianity have done the complete opposite of what people thought it was to do; hence, "Bass-Ackwards Society".

We all have freewill and the direction of our life is based on our experiences (lessons) and how we respond (emotions) to those experiences. We can continue to not address our emotions, blame others for how we feel, not learn from our experiences, and live an unhealthy life. We can continue to live "Inside a Box" where fear precedes any thought "Outside the Box". Where people have trouble forgiving and loving themselves; yes, this happens to be in the box too. Or we can address our emotions, shift our perspectives, learn from every experience, and live a healthy life. The choice has and will always be up to you, the individual with the perspective from the foundation.

www.ingramcontent.com/pod-product-compliance
Lightning Source LLC
Chambersburg PA
CBHW081454040426
42446CB00016B/3232